Isaac

Isaac

The Passive Patriarch

SHAUL BAR

WIPF & STOCK · Eugene, Oregon

ISAAC
The Passive Patriarch

Copyright © 2020 Shaul Bar. All rights reserved. Except for brief quotations in critical publications or reviews, no part of this book may be reproduced in any manner without prior written permission from the publisher. Write: Permissions, Wipf and Stock Publishers, 199 W. 8th Ave., Suite 3, Eugene, OR 97401.

Wipf & Stock
An Imprint of Wipf and Stock Publishers
199 W. 8th Ave., Suite 3
Eugene, OR 97401

www.wipfandstock.com

PAPERBACK ISBN: 978-1-5326-9419-6
HARDCOVER ISBN: 978-1-5326-9420-2
EBOOK ISBN: 978-1-5326-9421-9

Manufactured in the U.S.A.   01/07/20

Dedicated to the memory of
Bert Bornblum (1920–2016)
and
David Bornblum (1922–2004)

"…Beloved and cherished,
Never parted
In life or in death!" (2 Sam 1:23)

Contents

Acknowledgments	ix
Abbreviations	xi
Introduction	xv

1 | Abraham's Sons — 1
- The Birth of Ishmael — 2
- The Birth of Isaac — 8
- The Banishment of Ishmael — 12
- Ishmael Versus Isaac — 17

2 | The Binding of Isaac — 20
- Testing Abraham — 21
- Isaac in Light of the Akedah — 30
- The Purpose of the Story — 33

3 | A Wife for Isaac — 37
- Abraham and His Servant — 38
- The Servant and Rebekah at the Well — 40
- The Servant at Rebekah's House — 43
- Isaac and Rebekah — 47
- The Purpose of the Story — 49

4 | The Religious Customs in Isaac's Stories — 53
- Altars — 54
- Sacrifice — 56
- Prayers — 56
- Swearing — 58
- Blessing — 60
- Circumcision — 61

5	Whom Did Isaac Worship?	65
	The Worship of Elim	66
	Yahweh	68
	The God of My/Your/His Father	69
	Patron Deity	70
	Worshiping One God	72
	Theophany	73
	Angelology	77
6	Isaac at Gerar	80
	Descent to Gerar	81
	Digging Wells	87
	Isaac's Pact with Abimelech	89
	Similar Stories	92
	Structure and Setting of Chapter 26	95
7	Isaac's Wife-Sister	98
	A. Abraham in Egypt (Gen 12)	99
	B. Abraham in Gerar (Gen 20)	100
	C. Isaac in Gerar (Gen 26)	103
	Comparison of Story A and B	105
	Story C in comparison to A and B	106
	Story Repetition	109
8	Isaac and His Sons	113
	The Birth of Twins	114
	The Deception of Esau	117
	The Deception of Isaac	119
	The Death of Isaac	124
Conclusion		127
Bibliography		131
Index		139

Acknowledgments

To start with, I would like to thank my two readers who read the early drafts of the manuscript and offered many perceptive and insightful comments: Anna S. Chernak, who read the initial manuscript and offered valuable advice and continuous encouragement, and then Vivian Arendall, who made many suggestions and offered her wisdom.

I want to express appreciation to the staff of the Harding School of Theology in Memphis. Library director Bob Turner led me to many resources, Associate Librarian Sheila Owen helped me with research, and Don Meridith supported my efforts and inspired me.

Special thanks to Hebrew Union College Library in New York City, where Head Librarian Yoram Bitton provided me with help, wisdom, and friendship. Also, thank you to Librarian Tina Weiss who helped with my research.

Finally, a special thanks to the people at Wipf & Stock for their devotion and expertise in transforming my manuscript into this book.

SHAUL BAR
MEMPHIS, TN
JULY 2019

Abbreviations

AB	Anchor Bible
ABD	*The Anchor Bible Dictionary*. Edited by David Noel Freedman. 6 vols. New York: Doubleday, 1992.
ANET	*Ancient Near Eastern Texts Relating to the Old Testament: 3rd ed. with Supplement.* Edited by James B. Pritchard. Princeton: Princeton University Press, 1969.
AnBib	Analecta biblica
Ant	Josephus, Flavius. *Jewish Antiquities.* Translated by Henry St. John Thackeray. Cambridge, MA: Harvard University Press, 1930.
AOAT	Alter Orient und Altes Testament
AuOrSup	Aula orientalia, Supplementa
ASTI	*Annual of the Swedish Theological Institute*
b.	Babylonian Talmud
B. Bat.	Baba Batra
B. Meṣ.	Baba Meṣiʿa
BA	*Biblical Archaeologist*
BDB	Francis Brown, et al. *Hebrew and English Lexicon of the Old Testament.* Oxford: Clarendon, 1975.
BeO	*Bibbia e oriente*
Ber.	Berakot
BethM	*Beth Miqra: Journal for the Study of the Bible and its World*
BHS⁴	*Biblia Hebraica Stuttgartensia.* Edited by Karl Elliger and Wilhelm Rudolf. Stuttgart: Deutsche Bibelgesellschaft, 1997.

Abbreviations

Bib	*Biblica*
BibOr	*Biblica et Orientalia*
B. Kam.	*Baba Kamma*
BR	*Biblical Research*
BZAW	*Beihefte zur ZAW*
CBQ	*Catholic Biblical Quarterly*
DDD	*Dictionary of Deities and Demons in the Bible*. Edited by Karel van der Toorn, et al. Leiden: Brill, 1995.
EncJud	*Encyclopedia Judaica*. Edited by Fred Skolnik. 2nd ed. 22 vols. Jerusalem: Keter, 2007.
EM	*Encyclopedia Miqrait*
Exod. R.	*Exodus Rabbah*
Gen. R.	*Genesis Rabbah*
Giṭ.	*Giṭṭin*
HTR	*Harvard Theological Review*
HUCA	*Hebrew Union College Annual*
Ḥul.	*Ḥullin*
ICC	International Critical Commentary
IDB	*The Interpreter's Dictionary of the Bible*. 4 vols. Edited by George Arthur Buttrick. Nashville: Abingdon, 1962.
J. Ta'an.	*Jerusalem Ta'anit*
JBL	*Journal of Biblical Literature*
JEA	*Journal of Egyptian Archaeology*
JNES	*Journal of Near Eastern Studies*
JNSL	*Journal of Northwest Semitic Languages*
JSOT	*Journal for the Study of the Old Testament*
JSOTSup	Journal for the Study of the Old Testament Supplement Series
KAI	Herbert Donner and Wolfgang Röllig, *Kanaanäische und aramäische Inschriften*. 2nd ed. 3 vols. Wiesbaden: Otto Harrassowitz, 1967–1969.

Ket.	*Ketubbot*
Kid.	*Kiddushin*
KTU	*Die keilalphabetischen Texte aus Ugarit I.* Edited by Manfried Dietrich, et al. AOAT 24. Neukirchener-Vluyn: Neukirchener, 1976.
LAB	*Liber Antiquitatum Biblicarum*
Lev. R.	*Leviticus Rabbah*
LXX	Septuagint
Mak.	*Makkot*
2Mac	2 Maccabees
Mid.	*Middot*
Mish.	Mishnah
MK	*Moʿed Katan*
OBO	*Orbis Biblicus et Orientalis*
Pes.	*Pesaḥim*
PdRE	*Pirkei de-R. Eliezer*
PR	*Pesikta Rabbati*
PRU	*Le Palais royal d'Ugarit*
RHR	*Revue de l'histoire des religions*
Roš Haš	*RošHaššanah*
Ruth R.	*Ruth Rabbah*
Sanh.	*Sanhedrin*
SBLDS	Society of Biblical Literature Dissertation Series
Shab.	*Shabbat*
Šebu.	*Shevuʿot*
Tanḥ.	*Tanḥuma*
Tarbiz	*Tarbiz*
Targ. Onk.	Targum Onkelos

ABBREVIATIONS

TDOT	*Theological Dictionary of the Old Testament.* Edited by G. Johannes Botterweck and Helmer Ringgren. Translated by Geoffrey W. Bromiley. 14 vols. Grand Rapids: Eerdmans, 1974–2004.
TLOT	*Theological Lexicon of the Old Testament.* Edited by Ernst Jenni and Claus Westermann. Translated by Mark E. Biddle. 3 vols. Peabody, MA: Hendrickson, 1997.
Tosef.	Tosefta
VAB	*Vorderasiatische Bibliothek*
VT	*Vetus Testamentum*
VTSup	*VT* Supplement Series
Vulg	Vulgate
WBC	Word Biblical Commentary
WMANT	Wissenschaftliche Monographien zum Alten und Neuen Testament
Yev.	*Yevamot*
ZAW	*Zeitschrift für alttestamentliche Wissenschaft*

Introduction

Isaac, the second patriarch, son of Abraham and Sarah, was the child of a miracle at the time of his birth. His mother, Sarah, was barren until she was ninety years old, and his father one hundred years old. By the command of God he was named Isaac. He is the only patriarch who is mentioned by one name. He was forty years old when he married Rebecca (Gen 25:20). She was Isaac's sole wife in contrast to the other patriarchs who all had more than one wife. For twenty years the couple was childless. Finally, after God heard Isaac's prayers, Rebecca gave birth to twins: Esau and Jacob. When his sons were born Isaac was sixty years old.

An examination of the book of Genesis reveals that the stories about Isaac are found in:

1. Genesis 21:1–7, which describes the birth of Isaac.
2. Genesis 21:8–14 and 25:9–11, the stories about Isaac and Ishmael.
3. Genesis 22:1–19, the binding of Isaac.
4. Genesis 24:62–67, the meeting of Isaac and Rebecca.
5. Genesis 25:19–28, the birth of the twin brothers, Esau and Jacob, to Isaac and Rebecca.
6. Genesis 26, Isaac and the people of Gerar.
7. Genesis 27, Isaac's blessing of Jacob and Esau.
8. Genesis 35:27–29, the death of Isaac.

These stories are found only in seven chapters in the book of Genesis, but they also include stories about Abraham, Jacob, and Esau. In many instances the Isaac story is parallel to the Abrahamic tradition. Isaac, like his father Abraham, had feuds with Abimelech, passed his wife off as his sister, dug the wells that belonged to his father Abraham, and again gave them

Introduction

their original names. In other words, Abraham's history is repeated with Isaac; it is a copy of Abraham's stories, a mirror of his words and deeds. By Isaac following Abraham's footsteps the patriarchal history advances. He is the son of God's promise and is blessed with the Abrahamic blessing.

In most of the stories, Isaac is not the main character; he appears only as a secondary figure. He is mentioned with his father, Abraham, or with his sons, Jacob and Esau. The story of his birth and the promises that he received belong to the Abrahamic cycle. The blessings he received were the outcome of the blessings granted to his father. In the story of his binding, Isaac plays a passive role and this story is described best as the testing of Abraham. At the time of his marriage, again he is overshadowed by his father, Abraham, who sent the servant to bring Isaac a wife. In this story Isaac only welcomes his future wife—he is otherwise passive. With the birth of his sons, Esau and Jacob, the attention is shifted to the brothers and the rivalry between them. From this juncture, Jacob is the main character. Only in chapter 26 is the main focus on Isaac, who plays a leading role. The chapter is entirely devoted to him, as it describes Isaac's successes and his feuds with Abimelech. It paints a picture of Isaac's life in general.

Isaac lived in the southern part of Israel, in the Negev, near Beer-lahai-roi, and later, during the time of famine, he moved to Gerar. Though he was mistreated by the Philistines, he was blessed by God as an agriculturist and a cattle-breeder. In the end, he made a peace covenant with the Philistines at Beer-sheba, where he introduced the worship of Yahweh, who had appeared to him there. The last years of Isaac's life were hard after he became blind. Not knowing when he would die, he decided to give his blessing to his son Esau. Rebecca had other ideas, so with her orders, Jacob deceived his father and received the birthright for himself (27:1–29). This act increased the hostility between Isaac's sons, and led to Jacob's flight to Mesopotamia. Isaac lived to "a ripe old age" (35:27–29); he died when he was one hundred eighty years old, the longest any of the patriarchs lived. He was buried by his two sons at the cave of Machpelah beside his wife Rebecca (49:31).

Isaac's character appears to be less significant than that of his father or his sons. Not surprisingly, there are few details about him. He has no heroic traits and is described as a submissive person. He was lying passively when his father was going to sacrifice him. He did not go to find a wife, instead it was the servant who was sent to find a wife for him. In his dealings with the Philistines at first he appears as fearful (26:7–9). Later, in Genesis 27:33–37, when Jacob masquerades as Esau, he is portrayed as weak and easily persuaded. On the other hand, what we may perceive as weakness may have been his strength—he was patient and trusted God. He obeyed his father and pursued peace by giving in to the Philistines. He obeyed his wife and trusted her. He inherited and carried his father's spiritual mission which entailed obeying God and keeping his commandments, laws, and teachings (26:5). Isaac later left this heritage to his son Jacob. It is suggested that Isaac appears as less significant because he is the first one who attempted to settle and cultivate the land, a theme that is lacking with Abraham and Jacob.[1] It is difficult to accept this assertion since later the Israelites became farmers.

Outside of the Pentateuch, no independent tradition about Isaac is found. Therefore, it was thought that Isaac, like Abraham and Jacob, is an allegorical figure. His deeds reflect historical personalities of the monarchial period.[2] While the names Abraham and Jacob are found in extrabiblical secular documents, the name of Isaac has not been found outside of the Bible. This type of name beginning with a verb in the present or jussive form was a frequent form among the Amorites at the beginning of the second millennium. The name Isaac appears in the triad of Abraham, Isaac, and Jacob twenty-three times throughout the Pentateuch and seven times in the New Testament. Isaac's name is mentioned more than seventy times in Genesis, but only thirty-three times outside of that book. Indeed, the only places that there is independent tradition about Isaac is Genesis and the book of Amos. The prophet Amos mentions Isaac (yiśḥāq) as a synonym for Israel (7:9, 16). The spelling with ś instead of ṣ appears here twice. It also appears in Jeremiah 33:26 and Psalm 105:9 (1 Chr 16:16), which points to the fact that it is a legitimate variant. The pairing of Isaac and Israel is interesting. Isaac's connections are with the south and Israel refers to the Northern Kingdom, but Isaac is an alternate name for the Northern Kingdom. It is suggested that the prophet Amos mentions a special veneration for Isaac by the people of the Northern Kingdom; they made occasional pilgrimages south to Beersheba (5:5; 8:14), Isaac's birthplace.[3] Evidently, Isaac was an important figure during the Amos period. This leads us to believe that there existed more parallels between Isaac and the north, with more stories of Isaac existing, though subsequently have been lost.

---

1. Casuto, "Isaac," 753.
2. Sarna and Sperling, "Isaac," 33.
3. Hubbard, *Joel and Amos*, 210; van Selms, "Isaac in Amos," 160.

Introduction

The stories about the patriarchs probably originated in various ancestral groups which formed ancient Israel. The stories about Abraham and Isaac came from the southern part of Canaan where we read that both patriarchs were living in the region of Beer-sheba. On the other hand, the stories of Jacob came from the northern region since he lived in Bethel. The stories were linked together in order to create a record of successive generations of the family of Abraham's father, Terah of Ur. The short stories of Isaac were inserted between the more detailed stories of Abraham and Jacob. Isaac serves as a link between his father and son. According to Gunkel, Isaac has been described as a legendary figure,[4] while Eisfeldet describes him as a figure representing tribal history.[5] Alt sees Isaac as a seminomadic leader or founder of a cult.[6] Wellhausen suggests that where we have similar stories about Abraham and Isaac, the Isaac stories should be considered older and more original. The Isaac tradition, in particular, came from the earlier written source.[7] As Wellhausen says, "The short and profane version, of which Isaac is the hero, is more lively and pointed; the long and edifying version in which Abraham replaces Isaac, makes the danger not possible but actual, thus necessitating the intervention of the Deity and so brings about a glorification of the patriarch, which he little deserved."[8] He further says that Amos (earlier literature) mentioned Isaac, while Abraham appears only later in Isaiah 40–46.[9]

Noth maintained that the Isaac narrative is older than the West Jordanian Jacob narrative. It describes a period in which the Israelite tribes were not yet sedentary and were looking for grazing areas, when they had come into contact with the inhabitants of Southern Palestine.[10] According to Noth, the fact that there are similarities between the traditions of Isaac and Abraham shows that both figures were close to each other, spatially. He believes that Isaac was older than Abraham historically, but political factors such as Abraham in the south led to the understanding that he was the ancestor of the patriarchal tradition. In other words, Isaac lived prior to Abraham and was the more important icon. But it was only later in history

4. Gunkel, *Legends of Genesis*, 20.
5. Eissfeldt, "Palestine," 310
6. Noth, *History of Israel*, 121–27
7. Wellhausen, *Prolegomena*, 320.
8. Ibid., no. 1.
9. Ibid.
10. Noth, *History of Pentateuchal Traditions*, 106

INTRODUCTION

that Abraham took over the narrative elements.[11] According to Noth, Abraham took over when he became the predominant figure in the south. This view is not based on clear-cut verses, but is based on mere speculation. The order of the patriarchs is Abraham, Isaac, and Jacob, as it appears in the Hebrew Bible, and there is no compelling reason to change this order. The parallel stories about Abraham and Isaac are the result of a development of an early tradition that sometimes was attributed to one patriarch and sometimes to the other one. This duplication of the stories is natural to the book of Genesis, where some of the stories are repeated.

A different path was taken by Bright, who believes that Isaac, like his father Abraham, and his son Jacob, were actual historical individuals. He dismisses the notion that the patriarchs were a creation of legends, the eponymous ancestors of clans or reduced figures of gods. It is true that there are folkloristic motifs in the stories, but this belongs to the development of the narrative, not to its main characters, who are described most realistically.[12] The patriarchs were chiefs of large clans who were on the move. Most of our knowledge of the patriarchs comes from the Bible itself. Any attempt to rearrange these stories is moving us away from objective evidence. The stories were more complex than what we read in the Bible, but we have to rely on the Bible in order to trace the history of Isaac and pass judgment on him.

Surprisingly, there has not been a single comprehensive book about Isaac's entire life written so far, only those devoted to his binding story. What we do have are two dissertations which examine the Isaac story from a literary point of view: George Nicol's "Studies in the Interpretation of Gen 26:1–33," and David A. Lutz's "The Isaac Tradition in the Book of Genesis." In addition, we have commentaries on the book of Genesis. Through the years, important commentaries have been written on the book of Genesis. Among them are John Skinner's *A Critical and Exegetical Commentary on Genesis*, E. A. Speiser's *Genesis*, Claus Westermann's *Genesis 12–36*, and Nahum Sarna's *The JPS Torah Commentary: Genesis*.

In this book, our main goal is to rediscover Isaac, to have a better understanding of his personality, his achievements, and failures. We describe Isaac from different facets. In order to achieve this goal we will use the synchronic method, analyzing the chapters in the book of Genesis as they stand and comparing them to the other biblical texts and the Apocrypha.

11. Ibid., 103
12. Bright, *History of Israel*, 91–2.

Introduction

This, in turn, will shed more light on the persona of Isaac. Additionally, in order to have a better understanding into the Isaac cycle, material found in the Talmud, the Midrashim, and the Jewish medieval commentators will be reviewed. The Talmud contains a vast amount of *aggadot*—stories. The Midrash includes anthologies and compilations of homilies, including biblical exegesis and public sermons. The various sects and currents in Judaism left their mark on the Genesis stories, and almost everything that Jews thought during a period of more than one thousand years can be found there. Though the interpretative methods of the medieval commentators vary, we still can find that they compromise between the literal and the Midrashic interpretations of the biblical text. In addition, they pursue philological-contextual interpretations with a logical and scientific perspective.

In chapter 1 we study the birth story of Isaac, the son that Abraham waited for many years. An examination of this story shows that the narrator described the events that led to Isaac's birth in a detailed manner. The inevitable question that needs to be asked is: Why does the narrator attach such great importance to the description of Isaac's birth? And furthermore, by describing Isaac's birth, what was the author trying to achieve? Prior to the birth of Isaac we are told that Abraham already had a son named Ishmael through the maidservant Hagar. Thus, we will examine the Ishmael story and try to answer why the narrator included the Ishmael story. We compare Isaac's birth story to Ishmael's birth story. How similar are these stories, or how are they different? What was the narrator trying to express through these stories? Did the author want to point to the rivalry between the brothers, a theme which is prevalent in the book of Genesis, or to show the differences between the brothers? Alternatively, the author might have had some other considerations, such as a theological one for example, which he wanted to convey through the comparison between the two brothers.

Chapter 2 examines the story of the binding of Isaac. According to Genesis 22, God asked Abraham to sacrifice his son Isaac, the son he waited so many years for. Compliance to God's request meant an end to his future dreams with the nullification of the promises of posterity. God knows everything, so what was the purpose of putting Abraham through such an ordeal? We will analyze the characters of Abraham and Isaac in this story and see what we can learn about their personalities, especially concerning how Isaac is portrayed, in light of the Akedah, and how later generations perceived Isaac's persona.

INTRODUCTION

In chapter 3 we analyze Genesis 24. This chapter is the longest in the book of Genesis. It tells us about Abraham's servant who was sent on a mission to Mesopotamia to bring a wife for Isaac. We describe in minute detail the servant's meeting with Rebecca at the well, the repetition of this story to her family, the servant's negotiations with Rebecca's family, and finally the meeting between Rebecca and Isaac which leads to their marriage. We investigate the structure of the story and try to find out in what era this story was written. What kind of story is it? Why was this story formed, and what can we learn about Isaac's character?

The book of Genesis has neither laws nor moral responsibilities indicated. Only promises of nationhood and posterity were given to the patriarchs by God. Not surprisingly, some scholars claim there is no such thing as a patriarchal period or patriarchal religion. Indeed, in his *Prolegomena to the History of Israel*, published in 1878, Julius Wellhausen wrote that in Genesis there is "no historical knowledge of the patriarchs, but only of the time when the stories about them arose in the Israelite people; this later age is here unconsciously projected, in its inner and its outward features, into hoar antiquity, and is reflected there like a glorified mirage."[13] For this, chapter 4 examines some of the religious customs and practices that were already mentioned in the book of Genesis, such as: building altars, offering sacrifices, setting up pillars, swearing, praying, and circumcision. We compare these customs to later periods in the biblical narrative. This in turn helps us see if indeed the religious customs of the patriarch Isaac were authentic presentations of his faith or a presentation of religious beliefs from a later monarchial period.

In chapter 5 we look to answer the following questions: Whom did Isaac worship? Did Isaac worship Yahweh or did he worship other gods? To determine this, we examine the different names for God that appear in the Isaac stories. Names such as El Shaddai, El Elyon, El Olam, El Roi, El-elohei Israel, and El Bethel all will be discussed. In addition, we study the title "The God of my/your/his Father" and "the Fear of Isaac." How did God reveal himself to Isaac? Did God appear directly to Isaac or did he speak with him through the medium of dreams? Stories about angels' appearances to humans are typical to the patriarchal narrative and to the judges' period. In the Isaac and Ishmael stories angels are mentioned several times. However, the distinction between God and the angels is unclear in these stories, so was it God or an angel who revealed himself?

13. Wellhausen, *Prolegomena*, 318–19.

Introduction

Chapter 6 investigates Genesis 26, which contains the primary Isaac tradition. Isaac plays a major role in the story and the focus is centered on him in contrast to other stories where Isaac appears as a secondary character. This chapter describes Isaac's agricultural venture, his successes in digging wells, and his feuds with Abimelech the king of Gerar. In other words, it is the description of Isaac's life in general. Scholars point out that the stories of Abraham and Isaac overlap; their stories are mostly duplicates and their geographical spheres often coincide. Thus, we show how similar or different the stories are and what is the reason for this duplication. According to Noth, the stories in Genesis 26 are short stories which are united by the theme of Isaac and the people of Gerar. As mentioned before, he believes that Isaac was older than Abraham historically, but political factors, such as Abraham being from the south, led to the understanding that he was the ancestor of the patriarchal tradition. Thus, we will see if there is any validity to his suggestions. At first glance, chapter 26 looks out of place in the biblical narrative; it does not follow the chronological events which preceded it, therefore, we examine the setting of chapter 26 and its place in the book of Genesis. Furthermore, does this chapter contain a collection of originally independent traditions, or is it a coherent unit which requires a certain amount of inferred knowledge from the previous unit?

Chapter 7 compares the story of Isaac passing his wife Rebecca off as his sister to the two previous stories where the patriarch Abraham referred to his wife Sarah as his sister (12:10–20; 20). Furthermore, in chapter 20, the name of the king who was deceived is also Abimelek, the same king that Isaac deceived. These stories were believed to be three alternative folktales; however, there is no consensus among scholars which of the three represents the oldest form of the story. This chapter examines how similar or different the stories are. Why did the narrator repeat these stories? Repetition is a well-known technique that was used by the biblical narrator and is found in the literature of the ancient world. Did the narrator want to stress a point by repeating the stories while adding or subtracting details? Or did the repetition foreshadow future events?

Chapter 8 describes the last episodes of Isaac's life, which include the birth of his sons Esau and Jacob. What is behind this story? Was its purpose to describe the relationship between the two brothers? Or maybe the stories were created in order to explain the complex relationship between Israel and Edom in the later periods. Not knowing how soon he would die, Isaac felt the need to bless his son Esau. However, Jacob stole this blessing by tricking his brother Esau into selling his birthright and then deceiving his old and blind father, Isaac. We examine the blessings that Isaac bestowed on Jacob and Esau and see the differences between them. In addition, we answer why Jacob acted in such a deceitful and shameful manner, and whether he was punished for his acts. The death of Isaac is recorded in Genesis 35:27–29. He was buried by his sons Esau and Jacob: "He was gathered to his kin in ripe old age." What kind of message does the narrator try to convey by saying that Isaac was gathered to his kin? How should we view his life?

We trust that this study will provide a proactive and useful insight into the personality and life of the patriarch Isaac.

1

Abraham's Sons

Isaac, the long-promised son, was born to Abraham when he was one hundred years old and Sarah was ninety-one. However, he is not the firstborn son of Abraham. Sarah was barren so the matriarch resorted to the device of concubinage, giving her maidservant Hagar to Abraham. Examination of the social customs of the ancient Near East reveals that this was the norm and the respectable course of action. The union of Abraham and Hagar resulted in conception, and Ishmael was born. Abraham was eighty-six years old at that time. Eleven years had passed since his arrival in Canaan. Finally, after fourteen years of delay, Isaac, the promised son to Abraham and Sarah, was born (Gen 21:2). The book of Genesis describes the joyful and delightful events that led to the birth of Isaac. His name means "laughter," as explained in several episodes. Three times the Bible refers to the birth of Isaac (Gen 17:19; 18:12; 21:6) and all three occurrences connect his name with human laughter.

As Isaac grew and was weaned, Abraham held a great feast. During the celebration, Sarah saw Ishmael מצחק *měṣaḥēq* amusing himself, "playing" with Isaac. Sarah was seized with fear that the son of the concubine would inherit Abraham's heritage and not her own son. Therefore, she demanded that Hagar and her son be expelled. Abraham hesitated to comply with Sarah's request and only after God ordered him did he send Hagar and Ishmael into the desert. The scene of Hagar and her son going into the desert is very similar to a previous episode where Hagar ran away from Sarah to the desert. The main characters in these two stories are the same:

a jealous matriarch, a willing Abraham, and an Egyptian slave—Hagar. The birth story of Isaac is inserted between the two episodes which describe Hagar in the wilderness. It is noteworthy that we have a lengthy description leading to the birth of Isaac. This is in contrast to the birth of Abraham, where we were told in a single verse, "When Terah had lived seventy years, he begot Abram, Nahor and Haran," (Gen 11:26). Hence, we will examine the Hagar stories in the wilderness to see the similarities and differences between them. In addition, we will study the birth story of Ishmael and try to understand the reasoning behind its inclusion in the narrative, and why the biblical narrator went to such lengths to describe all the details that led to his birth and expulsion. This will lead us to scrutinize Isaac's birth story and compare it to Ishmael's birth story. How close or different are these stories? Did the author intentionally point out the theme of rivalry between the brothers, one which is so prevalent in the book of Genesis, or was it to show the differences between the brothers? Alternatively, the author had some other considerations, such as a theological one, which he wanted to convey through the comparison between the two brothers.

THE BIRTH OF ISHMAEL

When God elected Abraham, he promised him "I will make of you a great nation," (Gen 12:2). Still, years passed by and the promise of descendants remained unfulfilled. Throughout all the years, Abraham maintained his silence. However, in his first dialogue with God, which appears in "the covenant between the pieces" (Gen 15), Abraham complained to God that God did not grant him offspring of his own and instead it was his servant who would be his heir. Abraham referred to a custom which was prevalent in the ancient world in which a childless couple could adopt a person that would become their heir. In exchange, that unrelated person had to take care of the physical needs of the elderly couple.

To remove Abraham's doubts, God for the second time promised Abraham many descendants (15:5). In spite of God's promise of many descendants, we are told again that Abraham's wife, Sarah, had not borne him any children (17:1). The subject of Sarah's infertility was mentioned before when Terah took his family to go to Canaan (11:30). However, here we have a slight change; the narrator tells us that God kept Sarah from bearing (17:2), whereas before we were told that Sarah was barren. This change evidently stems from the narrator's knowledge of future events. The theme of barren women is a repeated motif in the Hebrew Bible. Hence, we read of the matriarchs Rebekah and Rachel, and later Samson's mother, and also Samuel's mother, Hannah, who were all barren.

Since the matriarch Sarah was a barren woman and God's promises remained unfulfilled, Sarah gave Hagar to her husband Abraham so they would have a son through her. How Sarah acquired Hagar we are not told. Therefore, it is possible that Hagar was probably among the servants that Abraham acquired during his stay in Egypt (Gen 12:16), or that she was part of Sarah's dowry.[1] Hagar was given to Abraham after he lived in Canaan for ten years. Therefore, according to the Talmud, if a man spent ten childless years with his wife, he could remarry, for he was not destined to have children by her.[2]

The purpose of marriage was procreation rather than companionship. Marriage contracts from the ancient Near East stipulate that a wife who failed to bear children had to provide her husband with a handmaid who would bear children for them. This practice of surrogate motherhood is attested to from the third to the first millennium BCE. For Sarah to give Hagar to Abraham so she would have a son through her was not unusual. The Code of Hammurabi makes a provision for a barren wife to give a slave to her husband so he can have children.[3] However, in this case it speaks about a priestess who was not permitted to have children. Documents from Nuzi attest to the practice of a barren woman giving her husband a secondary wife to bear a son who would become both the heir and the regarded son of the mother.[4] From Assyria, a marriage contract stipulates that the wife had to buy a slave for her husband if, after a period of two years, she could not give birth. When the slave girl had given birth, she was to be sold again.[5] In a document from Egypt, which dates to the first eighteen years of Ramses XI, we read about a couple without children that acquired a slave girl who then gave the husband three children, all of whom were adopted by the wife and therefore became legitimate.[6]

---

1. In the Aggadah, Hagar was the daughter of Pharaoh. After he witnessed the deeds performed on Sarah's behalf, in his house, Pharaoh gave Hagar to Sarah, saying: "Better let my daughter be a handmaid in this house than a mistress in another's" (*Gen. Rab.* 45:1).
2. *b. Yev.* 64a.
3. Meek, "Code of Hammurabi," 172n144, 172n147.
4. Gordon, "Biblical Customs," 1–12.
5. Finkelstein, "Additional Mesopotamian Legal Documents," 543n4.
6. Gardiner, "Adoption Extraordinary," 23–29.

At first glance, it appears the author of Genesis approved of Sarah's actions; however, it is more likely there is criticism toward Sarah. The matriarch does not wait for God's help but takes it upon herself to resolve the problem. This is a reminder of Abraham's previous behavior when, in times of crisis, he did not rely on God but passed his wife off as his sister. The wording of verses 2–3 suggests the narrator's disapproval, which clearly alludes to Genesis 3.

In the ancient world, barrenness was regarded as a disgrace. Thus, when Hagar became pregnant, her mistress was lowered in her esteem. According to Rashi (Rabbi Solomon ben Isaac, 1040–1105), Hagar was boasting to the ladies, "Since so many years have passed without Sarah having children, she cannot be as righteous as she seems. But I conceived immediately!" Similarly, we read in the midrash: "My mistress Sarah is not inwardly as she appears outwardly. She pretends to be a woman of piety, but she is not, as she has prevented conception in order to preserve her beauty."[7] According to Radak (Rabbi David ben Joseph Kimḥi, 1160–1235), since Hagar assured Abraham's posterity, she no longer felt subservient to Sarah.[8]

Hagar's attitude provoked Sarah's jealousy. Sarah appealed to God to judge between them. She refers to the wrong that was done to her as חמס *ḥamas*, a term used to describe the sins that prompted the flood (Gen 6:11, 13) and the vicious retaliation by Simeon and Levi (49:5; cf. 34:25). According to the midrash she was blaming Abraham: "You heard me insulted and did not speak up on my behalf."[9] Sarah was probably also afraid that her servant might usurp her place in Abraham's heart. She allowed Hagar to be an instrument of procreation but not to be a recipient of Abraham's feelings and love. Thus, she mistreated Hagar. The Hebrew verb ותענה *vatʿanneha* implies that Sarah subjected Hagar to physical and psychological abuse. Ramban (Rabbi Moses ben Naḥman known as Naḥmanides, 1194–1270), in his commentary, says, "The matriarch sinned by such maltreatment and Abraham too by permitting it." Abarvanel (Isaac ben Judah, 1437–1508), on the other hand, says that Sarah's intent was not malicious, but to force Hagar to cease her insulting demeanor. Instead of acknowledging Sarah's superior status, Hagar fled.

7. *Gen. Rab.* 45:4.

8. The Laws of Ur-Nammu deal with a similar situation when a female slave-concubine claimed equality with her mistress because she bore children: "If a man's slave women, comparing herself to her mistress, speaks insolently to her (or: him), her mouth shall be scoured with one quart of salt" (Finkelstein, "Laws of Ur-Nammu," 525n22).

9. *Gen. Rab.* 45:5.

Sarah treated Hagar harshly, so she fled into the wilderness of Shur, which is an area between Beer-sheba and Egypt. As she was passing a water spring, an angel of the Lord appeared to her. This is the first reference to "the angel of the Lord" in the Hebrew Bible, where it occurs forty-eight times—six of which happen in Genesis, with four instances occurring in chapter 16 (vv. 7, 9, 10, 11), and two related to the binding of Isaac (22:11, 15). The angel told Hagar that she was to bear a son. His name would be Ishmael and through him would come a multitude of descendants. Indeed, later we read that Ishmael became a father of twelve tribes (25:12–18). The name Ishmael means "God hears" because God heard Hagar in her affliction.[10] At first, she probably did not realize to whom she was talking but during the conversation she realized his identity. The "man" she met at the spring called her Hagar, slave of Sarah. Strangely, he knows her name but asks (v. 8), "Where have you come from, and where are you going?" This is evidently a rhetorical question the angel used to start the conversation with Hagar. It reminds us of God asking Adam "Where are you?" (3:9), and also when God asked Cain "Where is Abel" (4:9)? In contrast to Adam and Cain, who evaded and stalled, Hagar answered that she was running away from her mistress, Sarah. She does not respond to "Where are you going?," therefore it is possible she tried to avoid stating the fact that Egypt was her destination.

The angel told Hagar to return to her mistress and to submit to her harsh treatment. It appears that this command is a device used by the narrator to prepare the reader for the story of 21:9–21. In addition, since Hagar is not in mortal danger, the purpose of the appearance of the angel is to have Hagar return to Sarah. Hagar does not contest even though she knows that she will suffer. The commandment to submit to Sarah's harsh treatment does not coincide with verse 11, where it says that God has taken note of her suffering. Still, God is aware of her maltreatment and will compensate her. Indeed, the divine command is followed by the announcement that God will increase her offspring, which is like the promises to the patriarchs (Gen 17:2; 22:17; 26:24). Only after that is the reader informed of the birth of a son: "Behold, you are with child and shall bear a son; you shall call him Ishmael" (16:11).

The announcement of the birth of a son is also found in the Samson story. The angel appeared to Samson's mother and told her "but you shall conceive and bear a son" (Judg 13:3). Similarly, Mary, the handmaid of the

---

10. For more on the name of Ishmael see: Dahood, "Name *yišmāʿēl*," 87–88.

Lord, was told, "Behold you will conceive . . . and bear a son, and you shall call his name Jesus" (Luke 1:31). The announcement of the birth of a son usually follows a pattern which includes the announcement of the birth with a הנה *hinnēh* "behold" clause which is revealed to the father or mother. This is followed by the name of the child to be born and the nature and destiny of the child.

The future son of Hagar would be a wild ass of a man; in other words, he would be an undisciplined free man, which is the opposite of his mother.[11] This metaphorical use points to the nomadic lifestyle for Ishmael and his descendants. This way of life is found in Genesis 25:18, which describes the territorial boundaries of the Ishmaelites' confederation. According to Ibn Ezra (1089–1164), he would not submit to the rule of strangers and would take what he wanted by brutal force.

Hagar was so moved by her theophany experience, she called the lord who spoke to her "El Roi," which can be translated in various ways: "God of seeing" (Tg. Onk.); "God of my seeing" (Bekhor Shor, Joseph ben Isaac, 12th century; and Radak); and "God who sees me" (LXX, Vulg). According to Rashi, "The God of seeing" sees the humiliation of the humbled. Although an angel, and not God, spoke to her, she realized that it was God's emissary. Indeed, numerous emendations have been suggested to produce the sense or give it the meaning of: "You are a God of (my) seeing"; that is to say, "Did I really see God and have yet remained alive?"[12]

Hagar names the place *Beer-lahai-roi*. According to Sarna, the original meaning was: "the well belonging to the clan of Roi." In Arabic, ḥayy means "a clan," and Roi could be a proper name.[13] This, however, does not explain her experience; therefore it is more likely to mean "the well of the Living One who sees me."[14] Targum Onkelos translates it similarly: "the well where the living angel appeared." This new name of the place expresses her excitement and thanksgiving. Later the well became a place of prayer (Gen 24:62). According to Gunkle, the Bible describes legends about God and the tribal ancestor who met in a specific place. Jacob, for example, slept in a certain place resting his head on a stone while seeing the heavenly

---

11. A wild ass is an onager; unlike most horses and donkeys, onagers have never been domesticated. They are very fast, and their place of habitat is in waste places (Job 39:5–8; Isa 32:14; Jer 14:6; Hos 8:9).

12. Tsevat, *Meaning of the Book*, 63.

13. Sarna, *JPS Torah Commentary: Genesis*, 122.

14. Wenham, *Genesis 16–50*, 11.

ladder. Later this stone became a sanctuary (Gen 28:10–22). Similarly, the well in *lahai-roi* became a sanctuary for Ishmael because his mother met God at this well.[15] Another explanation might be that it is not Hagar who named the well. This is based on the fact that the verb קרא *qr'* "he called" is masculine singular. Therefore the subject could not be Hagar. According to *Midrash Sechel Tov*, it is Abraham in agreement with Hagar who gave it its name.[16] It is also possible that the descendants of Ishmael gave the spring this name when later they dug a well in the same place to commemorate the miracle that happened to Hagar.

Hagar accepted the words of the messenger, returned home, and bore a son to Abraham. The parenthood of the patriarch is mentioned three times (Gen 16:15–16). Furthermore, Abraham named the boy, and by doing so he recognized him as his legitimate son. Probably Hagar told him of her encounter with the angel, therefore he knew what to name his son.[17] Surprisingly, Sarah is not mentioned at all even though we would expect to find her in light of the prediction "Go back to your mistress" (v. 9). Hence, it is possible that Abraham protected Hagar.

The story of the birth of Ishmael in Genesis 16 is the opening event for the later story of the displacement of Ishmael.[18] As the reader recalls, we have already been told in 15:3–4 that a slave is not to be Abraham's heir. In that chapter, Abraham's complaint was about Eliezer Damascus which, according to Thompson, prepares the reader for the greater story of the displacement of Ishmael.[19] The story of the birth of Ishmael is a delay in God's promise to Abraham for a son and heir. The son of a slave woman cannot be his true heir or his true son. This ultimately will be changed with the birth of Isaac. Similarly, Benno Jacob says that the story about Ishmael is a necessary part of Abraham's story. Abraham shall have a son and heir; however, his birth by Sarah is delayed so that it will be more appreciated.[20] The birth of Ishmael is a result of human interference as it was the outcome of Sarah giving Abraham her concubine, Hagar. The matriarch does not wait for God's help but takes it upon herself to solve the problem. Isaac, on the other hand, as we shall see below, was born as a result of God's involvement.

15. Gunkel, *Legends of Genesis*, 33.
16. *Midrash Sechel Tov*, 11.
17. Jacob, *First Book of the Bible*, 107.
18. Thompson, *Origin Tradition of Ancient Israel*, 90.
19. Ibid.
20. Jacob, *First Book of the Bible*, 107

Isaac

THE BIRTH OF ISAAC

Abraham was promised many descendants, though this promise was made without any explanation as to how it would materialize. However, in Genesis 17:16, for the first time the reader is informed that it will be through Sarah. Noteworthy, in the previous verse Sarai's name is changed to Sarah. From this verse the sages concluded that a change of name brings a change of man's faith.[21] According to Ralbag (Rabbi Levi ben Gershom, known as Gersonides, 1248–1344) after Sarah's name was changed she was blessed with a son. The Bible records Abraham's reaction, which has two parts: he threw himself on his face and then laughed. This act is an expression of reverence, or according to Radak it can be an indication of gratitude for the good news concerning Sarah. Abraham's laughter is a sign of his future son's name. The Hebrew word ויצחק *vyiṣḥāq and laughed* also spells *and Isaac*. The laughter can be explained as disbelief since, at that time, the patriarch was one hundred years old and his wife was ninety. Alternatively, the laughter here is an expression of joy. God told Abraham that he should name his son Isaac as he would be the heir to the Abrahamic covenant with God—an everlasting covenant between God and Isaac and his offspring to come.

Three times the Bible refers to the birth of Isaac (17:19; 18:12; 21:6), and in these three occurrences the name is connected with human laughter. When Sarah was inside the tent and heard about the birth of her son, she laughed to herself. The Bible tells us that she was old and she stopped having her menstrual cycle. Indeed, in three separate occasions there is a reference to the old age of Abraham and Sarah (18:11, 12, 13). The narrator calls both of them "elderly." Evidently this laughter of Sarah is the result of skepticism in light of her advanced age. Sarah's laughter will turn to a joyous laugh after she gives birth (21:6). It is suggested that the original name of Isaac is Isaac-el "El laughs." The name consists of an imperfect verb and divine name which is also found in names such as Ishmael and Israel. The subject of the verb צחק *sḥq* is the deity, not the father or the child. Hence, Isaac el would mean "El smiles" or "El is favorable." Support for this can be found in Ugaritic texts where the god El is said to smile in expressing his favor or satisfaction.[22] However, we should point out that this form "Isaac-el" is not found in the Hebrew Bible nor any proper name with this stem.

---

21. *Roš Haš.* 16b.
22. Stamm, "Der Name Isaak," 35.

Abraham's reaction to the announcement of the birth of Isaac is quite puzzling: "O that Ishmael might live by Your favor" (17:18). According to Rashi, Abraham's response has two parts: 1) I am unworthy of a great reward as to have a son now, and 2) it will suffice if only Ishmael lives righteously before you. Ramban (Rabbi Moses ben Naḥman, known as Naḥmanides, 1194–1270) has a different explanation; according to him, Abraham feared that the birth of Isaac as his true heir might signal Ishmael's death, so he prayed for his life. Furthermore, it appears that God's words excluded the boy from the covenant. Abraham loved his son Ishmael and did not want to lose him. Clines suggests that Abraham's reaction shows that he does not believe in this future son and that he is perfectly content with Ishmael.[23] For Abraham, Ishmael is the fulfillment of the promise of an heir, a son of his own loin that was circumcised according to the covenant. God promised Abraham that he would be a father of a multitude of nations (17:4–6). Abraham thought that Lot and Ishmael were the fulfillment of God's promise, but for God it was Isaac who would carry the Abrahamic promises.

In Genesis 15:4, God tells Abraham that his heir will be a natural-born son, while Genesis 17:16–21 states that Sarah would be the mother of his child. Finally a specific time is set: "I will return to you next year, and your wife Sarah shall have a son" (18:10)! This announcement by the angels of the birth of a son is similar to the previous announcement to Hagar by an angel. God's promise will materialize, as we are told "The Lord took note of Sarah as he had promised and the Lord did for Sarah as he had spoken" (21:1). The fulfillment of the promise is mentioned twice in the verse in order to stress that God's promise came to fruition. The narrator uses the verb פקד *pkd* "took note" to describe God's visitation to Sarah. The same expression "took note" also appears in Samuel's birth story.[24] It is suggested that this phrase appears when the infant is a child of destiny. The verb *pkd* is mentioned in the Hebrew Bible when God is directly involved in human affairs. This verb appears as a recurring motif of divine promises of a national redemption from Egyptian slavery (Gen 50:24–25; Exod 4:31); to end famine (Ruth 1:6); and to bring the exiles home (Jer 29:10).[25] Alternatively, *pkd* is used when a husband visits his wife for sexual purposes (Judg 15:1). In other words, our story is a myth about Isaac's divine paternity. In the ancient world, various myths about sexual relations between gods and

23. Clines, *What Does Eve Do?*, 75.
24. Sarna, *JPS Torah Commentary: Genesis*, 145.
25. Wenham, *Genesis 16–50*, 80.

daughters of men were prevalent. As a result of these unions the children that were born were half gods or were raised to the status of deities. Thus, it is possible that the story of the birth of Isaac follows this pattern. However, we believe that our story is about divine mercy, how God delivers one from a hard situation like infertility.

Sarah conceived as promised and bore a son to Abraham. The Bible mentions Abraham's advanced age: he was one hundred years old, which stresses the late arrival of his heir. It is a late gift by God. This is a typical folk motif which describes the divine promise of a son to an elderly couple. Indeed, in the story about the Shunammite woman we read that her husband is old, similar to the words that described Abraham (2 Kgs 4:14). In the same way, in the New Testament, Elizabeth was barren and she and her husband Zachariah were old (Luke 1:7). These stories share a basic structure: 1) Mention of infertility, 2) the prediction of childbirth at a set time, and 3) the fulfillment of the promise as foretold.

Did Sarah become pregnant after the incident in Gerar or before? Did a year pass from Genesis 17:21 ("But my covenant I will establish with Isaac, whom Sarah shall bear to you at this season next year") until Isaac's birth in 21:2? Or did nine months pass from Genesis 18:10 ("I will surely return to you next year") to the birth of Isaac in 21:2? Was Isaac born after the story in Genesis 20 about Abimelech? In that story Abraham referred to his pregnant wife as his sister.[26] Clines suggests that at the beginning of chapter 20 Abraham still does not believe in Yahweh's promise of Isaac. If he really believed God he would know that the child to be born is in danger, just like his mother. Another question that needs to be asked: What was Abraham doing at Gerar since there is no mention of famine? He puts his family in unnecessary danger.[27]

To remove any suspicion that Abraham is not the father of Isaac because Abimelech took Sarah to his harem, the author repeats twice that Abraham is the father of Isaac: "This is the story of Isaac, son of Abraham. Abraham begot Isaac" (Gen 25:19). This kind of usage is not found in אלה תולדות *'elleh toledot* "This is the story." However, later the chronicler used the same pattern to record that the sons of Abraham were Isaac and Ishmael (1 Chr 1:28), and then again said that "Abraham begot Isaac" (v. 34). Evidently, what the author wanted to emphasize was that Abraham is the father of Isaac, who is the sole successor to the Abrahamic covenant.

---

26. Clines, *What Does Eve Do?*, 75–76.
27. For more on these subjects, see ch. 7.

Rashi, in his commentary on verse 19, says that there was a need to repeat twice that Abraham is the father. Scorners of that generation were saying "From Abimelech did Sarah conceive since for many years she tarried with Abraham and did not conceive from him." What did the Holy One, Blessed be He, do? He formed the features of Isaac's face similar to Abraham and there attested everyone, "Abraham begot Isaac." And that is why it is written here, "Isaac was the son of Abraham," for there is testimony that "Abraham begot Isaac."[28]

When Isaac is born, Abraham names his son as he was told to do by God (Gen 17:19). Because his name is fixed by God, Isaac is the only patriarch whose name was not changed. God revealed his name before he was born. Abraham circumcised him on the eighth day as set out in 17:12. Isaac is the first person that was circumcised on the eighth day, in contrast to Ishmael who was circumcised when he was thirteen. This detail comes to emphasize that Isaac is the true heir to the Abrahamic covenant. Abraham was one hundred years old when his son Isaac was born. This statement by the narrator links the narrative to Abraham's previous statement: "Can a child be born to a man a hundred years old" (17:17)? Surprisingly, we do not find any emotional reaction by Abraham at the birth of his son. On the other hand, the matriarch's reaction is recorded. Sarah breaks into laughter; this is a joyous laughter in contrast to her earlier laughter of disbelief. She utters a short song: a poetic cry of joy that contains three lines with three Hebrew words in each:

> "Who would have said to Abraham
> That Sarah would suckle children!
> Yet I have borne a son in his old age." (21:7)

According to Sarna, the forms of the verb and the stem מלל *m-l-l* seem to indicate that Sarah uttered an ancient poem.[29] It is suggested that "it is an ancient traditional form of informing the father: Sarah suckles a child![30] The second part of the announcement mentioned the cry of joy: I have born my husband a son in his old age! The last sentence (6b) refers to the surprise of others: everyone who hears will laugh with me.[31] It is suggested

---

28. See also *b. B.Meṣ.* 87a.
29. Sarna, *JPS Torah Commentary: Genesis*, 146.
30. Westermann, *Genesis 12–36*, 334.
31. Ibid.

this call to celebrate over the birth of the rightful heir was meant to insult Hagar and her son.[32]

Abraham held a great feast on the day Isaac was weaned. This normally occurred at the age of two or three (1 Sam 1:22–24; Hos 1:8). In Egypt and Assyria, breast-feeding frequently lasted three years; this was also a prevalent practice in Israel during Second Temple times.[33] One statement in the Talmud limits the practice to twenty-four months, while another refers to a period of four or five years.[34] It was a family feast that celebrated an important event that the child passed the first stage of his life.

The celebration was interrupted when Sarah saw Ishmael playing. The meaning of the word playing מצחק *metsaḥek* is not clear so it was given a different interpretation.[35] The LXX and Vulgate added "with her son Isaac" after playing. Thus, the question arises: Was Ishmael playing innocently with Isaac or abusing him? Paul, in his writings, suggests that Ishmael was "persecuting" (edíōken) Isaac (Gal 4:29). This can mean verbal or physical, as in sexual abuse. In the book of Jubilees, we find a different interpretation: "Sarah saw Ishmael playing and dancing, and Abraham rejoicing with great joy, and she became jealous of Ishmael" (Jub. 17:4). Ralbag pointed out that Ishmael mocked the great feast since he was also Abraham's son but there was no feast when he was weaned. According to Benno Jacob, Ishmael boasted of his earlier birth just like his mother did (16:4).[36]

THE BANISHMENT OF ISHMAEL

The scene of Ishmael playing with Isaac was too much for Sarah. Therefore, she demanded that Abraham drive out Hagar and Ishmael. The narrator uses the verb גרש *gāraš*, which is the same verb that describes the banishment of Adam and Cain from the garden of Eden (Gen 3:24; 4:14). This verb is also used in the Bible as a term for divorce (Lev 21:7, 14; 22:13), which is evidently implied here too. When Abraham later sent Hagar away, the Bible uses the verb שלח *shillaḥ*, which is used for divorce as well as the release of slaves (Deut 22:19, 29; 24:1, 3; Jer 34:9, 16; Mal 2:16). Sarah's forcefulness and determination are revealed in the expulsion of Hagar and her son.

32. Mathews, *Genesis*, 268.
33. 2Mac 7:27.
34. *b. Ket.* 60a; *b. Git.* 75b.
35. Pinker, "Expulsion of Hagar and Ishmael," 3–6.
36. Jacob, *First Book of the Bible*, 137.

Ishmael was a legitimate son of Abraham and was entitled to the rights of inheritance. However, Sarah wanted the line of Abraham to continue only through her son Isaac. Thus, she demanded that Abraham cast out the slave-wife and her son. Though Ishmael is the main character in the story, he is not mentioned by name through the whole account. By not mentioning Hagar and Ishmael's names, Sarah was belittling them. The matriarch did not have any relationship with Hagar and she did not have any interest in Hagar's son. Sarah did not want Isaac and Ishmael to share Abraham's inheritance. Children that were born to a slave-wife could inherit along with the children of the primary wife.[37] The laws of Lipit-Ishtar indicate that the father may grant freedom to the slave-woman and her children, and by doing so they would forfeit their share of the paternal property.[38] Sarah was not afraid of the division of the inheritance; what she feared was Ishmael. She was afraid that his physical powers and seniority would drive Isaac away and Ishmael would seize the entire inheritance for himself.

Sarah's demand was very painful for Abraham, who became distressed. Abraham considered Ishmael his son. The fact that he rejected his son in this fashion does not bode well with Abraham as a moral man. It was only after God confronted him that he complied with Sarah's request. The line of Abraham would continue through Isaac. God referred here to Ishmael as "the youth" rather than "your son." Later, in verse 14, when Abraham fulfills God's order to expel Ishmael and Hagar, he refers to Ishmael as "the boy" rather than "my son."

God told Abraham to listen to Sarah. In many biblical texts, important decisions about family, children, and succession were determined by the women. This is evident here with Sarah and later with Rebekah. God told Abraham to heed Sarah and trust her judgment because, as a woman, she had deeper insight of character than he did. It was Sarah's vision and foresight that determined the continuity of the family. Here, Abraham is subordinate to Sarah. The sages pointed out that the patriarchs were dependent on the superior powers of the matriarchs. They said that Sarah possessed prophetic powers and was one of the seven prophetesses, and her prophetic gifts were even superior to Abraham's.[39] Since Abraham loved his son Ishmael, God reassured Abraham that no harm would befall Hagar

---

37. Fensham, "Son of a Handmaid," 312–21; Thompson, *Historicity of the Patriarchal Narratives*, 263–67.
38. Kramer, "Lipit–Ishtar Law Code," 160n25.
39. *Exod. Rab.* 1:1.

and Ishmael in the wilderness. Ishmael was a descendant of Abraham with a great future awaiting him, and he would be rewarded with greatness and would also become a nation (Gen 21:13). This blessing is a repetition of the former blessing that God promised Abraham about Ishmael: ". . . and I will make him a great nation" (Gen 17:20). These promises are similar to promises that were given to the patriarchs.

Early in the morning Abraham took bread and the water container, giving them to Hagar. He did it early in the morning since he probably wanted to do it privately. He was reluctant to send Hagar with his son and did not want to show any emotion in the presence of his wife, Sarah. He supplied Hagar with basic provisions, which is quite puzzling. Calvin is baffled by Abraham's behavior:

> "But with how slender a provision (*tenui . . . viatico*) does he endow his wife and son? He places a flagon of water and bread upon the shoulder. Why does he not load an ass, at least, with a moderate supply of food? Why does he not add one of his servants, of which his house contained plenty, as a companion?[40]

Was it Abraham's secret intention to make sure Hagar could not go too far? The fact that Hagar was able to carry the boy, bread, and water sack, shows that Abraham indeed gave her very little. According to Calvin, Abraham's treatment of Hagar and Ishmael is the result of pride and ingratitude:

> "God willed that the banishment of Ishmael should be so harsh and sorrowful (*tam dura et tristis*), so that his example might strike terror into the proud, who. . .trample under the foot the very grace to which they indebted for all things. Therefore, he led them both to a miserable end."[41]

Cohen, on the other hand, sees in Abraham's behavior an expression of his total faith in God: "Convinced that God had great, though awesome, plans for Ishmael, Abraham was in no way callous in sending the young Ishmael off into the desert with only his mother to protect him. As far as Abraham was concerned, his son had a far greater Protector than his mother to secure his safety."[42] Nikaido, meanwhile, suggests that "The meager

---

40. Calvin, *Commentaries on the First Book*, 548; Thompson, "Hagar, Victim or Villain?," 223.

41. Calvin, *Commentaries on the First Book*, 548; Thompson, "Hagar, Victim or Villain?," 223.

42. Cohen, "Was Abraham Heartless?," 181.

supply of provisions (contrast Gen 25:6) given to Hagar and her infant son for a grueling trek through the desert (cf. Exod 15: 22f) conveys a clear message: Ishmael is not the heir—not anyone's heir."[43]

Hagar probably went toward her native Egypt, but she lost her way in the wilderness of Beer-sheba. When the water supply was gone, Hagar left her son under one of the bushes so at least he would be protected from the sun. She was anticipating his death as she could not prevent it. To avoid seeing his death and hearing his cries, she sat at a distance. The distance is described as a bowshot away which alludes to Ishmael's later profession as a bowman (Gen 21:20). Hagar was crying and so was Ishmael. God heard Ishmael's cries in light of his promises to Abraham. It is God who hears the cries of the boy, but it is the angel of God who called Hagar. The mention that *God heard* further explains the name "Ishmael," which was given in chapter 16. As noted previously, this chapter never mentions—not even once—the name Ishmael, instead he is described as "son," "lad," or a "child." As Wenham points out, the cryptic reference to Ishmael's name is meant to recall his origin, "You shall name him Ishmael, for the Lord has noticed your oppression" (16:11).[44] The promise given to Abraham in verse 13, that Ishmael would become a great nation, is repeated here (v. 18), because in verse 13 it was only Abraham who heard it. Now it has to be repeated to Hagar since she now takes the place of his father Abraham.

The two stories about Hagar in 16:1-4 and 21:8-21 contain many similar details. The main characters are the same: a jealous matriarch, a willing Abraham, and the Egyptian slave, Hagar. The jealousy of Sarah is mentioned in both stories and Abraham's reaction is similar, namely, he accommodated Sarah's request. In both stories Hagar leaves and goes into the wilderness. In the wilderness, God reveals himself at the well and delivers a message of encouragement and posterity. It is because both accounts contained common features, that it has been suggested that they were alternate accounts of the same incident.[45] In spite of the common motifs in 16:1-16 and 21:1-21, there are still some differences between the two stories. In the first story Hagar runs away from Sarah; in the second story she is banished. In chapter 16, there is rivalry between the barren Sarah and her pregnant maidservant; but in chapter 21, the main issue is a conflict over the inheritance. In chapter 16, Hagar knows her way; in chapter 21, she loses her way.

---

43. Nikaido, "Hagar and Ishmael," 224.
44. Wenham, *Genesis 16–50*, 85.
45. Skinner, *Genesis*, 159; Speiser, *Genesis*, 156.

Isaac

In the first story God hears of the mistreatment of Hagar; in the second he hears the crying of the boy. In the first story the unborn child receives his name and so the well also gets a name; in the second story there is no mention of the boy's name or that of the well. In the first story Hagar sees the well; in the second the angel has to open her eyes in order to see the well. In the second story Hagar is in great distress; while in the first one she takes the initiative and runs away.[46]

To solve the literary and chronological difficulties in the texts, modern scholars who adhere to the documentary hypothesis assign the first tradition about Hagar (16:1–14) as predominantly J, with P inserting verses 1a, 3, 15–16; the second story (21:1–21) is entirely E. In other words, there were two stories of the banishment of Hagar—one before her pregnancy and a second one after the birth of Isaac. To resolve the assumed conflation, it was suggested that 16:9 was a late redaction whose purpose was to give sequence to the narrative. Another suggestion was that the naming of Ishmael was deleted in the second story. However the attempt for assigning these narratives to different sources proves to be unconvincing. As Speiser notes, "The various emendations that have been proposed merely substitute one set of problems for another. An acceptable solution has yet to be discovered."[47] More than likely the stories have an etiological purpose which is to explain the name Ishmael. Therefore, the root שמע šmʿ is repeated in the two chapters. The verb šmʿ is part of the name Ishmael. Abraham heeds (šmʿ) Sarah's request when she offers him her maid (16:2). The angel tells Hagar that she will call her son Ishmael because "the Lord has paid heed (šmʿ) to your suffering" (16:11). When Sarah requests Abraham to expel Hagar, God tells Abraham "whatever Sarah tells you do as she says (šmʿ)" (21:12). When Hagar loses her way in the desert the text says: "God *heard* the cry of the boy...God *heeded* (šmʿ) the cry of the boy" (21:17). The stories serve as an etiology of the Ishmaelite-Hagarite tribes and to explain Ishmael's presence in the wilderness. These stories were linked to the theme of Isaac. However, this combination created chronological problems which did not exist when these traditions were independent. According to Genesis 16:16, Abraham was eighty-six years old at the birth of Ishmael and one hundred years old when Isaac was born (21:5), this would make Ishmael more than fourteen years old when he was expelled (21:10–19). To

---

46. On the differences between the texts see: Alexander, "Hagar Traditions," 132–33; Neff, "Annunciation in the Birth Narrative," 51–60.

47. Speiser, *Genesis*, 155.

resolve the account for this merging of the texts it was suggested that the banishment account of Hagar and her younger son was combined with the story of the birth of Isaac in Abraham's old age.

ISHMAEL VERSUS ISAAC

The stories of the birth of Ishmael and Isaac come to show the differences between the two brothers. Ishmael is a hunter, while Isaac, as the reader will discover later, was quite a peaceful tent-dweller. Ishmael's story explains etiologically how Ishmael received his name and became a Bedouin. It describes the nature of the Ishmaelites as a wild nomadic people who roamed the desert between Israel and Egypt, as it says, "He shall be a wild ass of a man; his hand against everyone. And everyone's hand against him; he shall dwell alongside of all his kinsmen" (Gen 16:12). Hunting is not mentioned much in the Hebrew Bible. The only hunters who are mentioned are Nimrod ("a mighty hunter" Gen 10:9); Ishmael ("a bowman" Gen 21:20); and Esau, who is described as going to the field with quiver and bow (Gen 27:2). The Bible held hunting in low esteem and has a negative attitude toward hunting as a way of life. Much of Near Eastern art portrays kings as engaged in hunting, but not so the Israelites or Judean kings. The animals that the Israelites used for sacrifice were restricted to domesticated animals.[48] By describing Ishmael as a hunter, the biblical narrator shows his contempt toward Ishmael. In other words, he is not worthy of being Abraham's heir, so it is the second son who would become the next patriarch. It is notable that in the Hebrew Bible we have many examples of the younger brother replacing the older brother. The first example is Isaac and Ishmael, but later on there are Jacob and Esau, Zerah and Perz, Ephraim and Manasseh, David and his older brothers, as well as Solomon and Adonijah.

The insertion of the Hagar-Ishmael stories has one purpose: to show that Isaac is the true heir to Abraham. It comes to stress the supremacy of the Israelites over the Ishmaelites who also trace their lineage through Abraham. Isaac is the son of the chief wife/matriarch and Ishmael is the son of an Egyptian maidservant. The banishment of Ishmael in Genesis 21 serves three functions.[49] First, it allows Isaac to replace Ishmael as the true heir of Abraham as promised in the stories in Genesis 15 and 16. Second, it prepares the reader for Genesis 21, which knows nothing about Abraham's

---

48. Sarna, *Understanding Genesis*, 181.
49. Thompson, *Origin Tradition of Ancient Israel*, 96.

Isaac

son Ishmael and sees only Isaac as the only *begotten son*. And finally, it also brings the story of Ishmael to a close in light of Genesis 17:4–6; in those verses Abraham is understood to be the father of many nations, not just Israel and Ishmael. Like Isaac, Ishmael is to be made into a nation; a great future awaits him. Ishmael is to become the father of twelve tribes (16:10). He is circumcised according to the covenant with Yahweh (17:7, 23). However there is a major difference between the brothers which is that "in Isaac shall your descendants be called" (21:12).

The fact that Isaac is the true heir and successor to Abraham is borne out in the following passage: "Abraham willed all that he owned to Isaac" (Gen 25:5). Abraham had many sons besides Ishmael and Isaac, thus, to remove any questions as to the status of Isaac, we are told of the measures that were taken by Abraham: "but to Abraham's sons by the concubines Abraham gave gifts while he was still living, and he sent them away from his son Isaac eastward, to the land of the East" (25:6). In this era the patriarch could designate his successor regardless of the order of his sons' births which is in contrast to later legislation of the Torah (Deut 21:15–17). First, Isaac is acknowledged as the sole heir of Abraham. Second, Abraham also gave gifts to his other sons, which could be interpreted as generosity on Abraham's part, in order to ensure peaceful relations between the other sons and Isaac. Third, he *sent* the sons of the concubines to the lands of the East. The term *send* was used already to describe the expulsion of Hagar and Ishmael. Our verse is essentially the same as 24:36. There we read that the servant stated that Abraham gave all his possessions to Isaac. Ramban, in his commentary on 24:10, says that our verse (25:6) means that Isaac had already taken possession of Abraham's property so that at the time of his death, the other children would not contest his ownership. It is noteworthy that most of Abraham's assets went to Isaac, while Ishmael is not even mentioned.

In conclusion, Abraham was promised to have many descendants, but without any details or explanation as to how it would materialize. The births of his two sons, Ishmael and Isaac, are the fulfillment of God's promises. However, the birth of Ishmael is the result of human interference; it was the outcome of Sarah giving Abraham her concubine, Hagar. Isaac, on the hand, was born as a result of God's involvement. The stories come to explain the origin of the Ishmaelites and Israelites. It explains the nature of the Ishmaelites as a wild nomadic people who roamed the desert between Israel and Egypt. The story of the banishment of Ishmael comes to legitimize Isaac as the true heir to the Abrahamic covenant. Through Isaac the line of Abraham would continue.

Interestingly, the next story that mentions Isaac is "the binding of Isaac." Abraham waited many years for the birth of Isaac, and then he was told by God to sacrifice him. Hence, in the next chapter we will examine the story of the binding of Isaac and try to understand the purpose of this story. In addition, we will examine the character of Isaac in light of this ordeal which resulted from God's request.

2

The Binding of Isaac

THE FIRST EPISODE ABOUT the life of the patriarch Isaac is the story of his binding. In Genesis 21, we were told about his birth and the great feast that Abraham held the day that Isaac was weaned. Now, in chapter 22, we read that God asked Abraham to sacrifice his son Isaac, a son he had waited so many years for. There is not a single word about Isaac's youth, which is similar to what happens with the story of Abraham. Compliance with God's request means an end to his future dreams and nullification of the promises of Abraham's posterity. This story is the climax of Abraham's religious odyssey and the ultimate trial of his faith. However, a question needs to be raised here: Why does God need to test Abraham? God knows everything. In this chapter we will try to explain the reasoning behind the test. Different interpretations are given as to the nature of this test. It is believed that the story is an etiological legend. It came to explain why the custom of the sacrifice of a child at a certain place was substituted by a ram. In other words, it is a story of the transition from human sacrifice to animal sacrifice. Therefore, we will examine whether this is indeed the case and, if so, what is the reason behind it. In addition, we will study the different interpretations that are given to this story. This endeavor will help us to scrutinize the character of Isaac in light of this horrific story. What can we learn about Isaac's conduct before and after this ordeal? Additionally, how was the persona of Isaac perceived in later writings? Was Isaac a willing victim, or did he resist his father? In order to answer these and other questions we will analyze the

THE BINDING OF ISAAC

story through a close reading of the biblical text and explore the postbiblical texts that are relevant to our study.

TESTING ABRAHAM

The story starts with the introduction that God tested Abraham. Testing is found in other instances in the Hebrew Bible. For example, God tested the Israelites in the wilderness (Exod 15:25; 16:4; Deut 8:2, 16), and tested Job. Job's devotion to God was called into question by Satan (Job 1:9). This resulted in suffering that included the loss of his children. Abraham and Job, both survived the test and were found to be "God-fearing" men (Gen 22:12; Job 1:9). They complained about divine justice, with Abraham saying, "Shall not the judge of all earth deal justly?" (Gen 18:25), and Job saying, "Will the Almighty prevent justice" (Job 8:3)?

The fact that Abraham is given a test is revealed at the outset of the story to the reader, but not to Abraham. It comes to remove any impression that God requires human sacrifice. The reader knows that his son will not be slaughtered. Thus, the question that is left to the reader is will Abraham comply with God's request or will his love for his son prevent him from submitting to God's command?

Before receiving God's command, Abraham uttered one word, הנני *hinneni*, "Here I am," which expresses attentiveness. This is the only word that Abraham says to God in the whole story. Earlier in the story of Sodom and Gomorrah, Abraham intercedes on behalf of total strangers to save their lives. Here when he received the command from God to sacrifice his own son he did not plead for his son's life nor did he try to save him. The single Hebrew word "Here I am" appears again in the text when Isaac turned to his father with a question and Abraham replied, "Here I am" (Gen 22:7). Similarly, when the angel of the Lord called Abraham from heaven, the patriarch answered, "Here I am" (v. 11). Three times the name of the patriarch "Abraham (my father)" is mentioned (vv. 1, 7, 11) before being followed by the response, "Here I am." Each points to a new development in the narrative.[1]

When God told Abraham, "Take your son," the Hebrew adds the particle נא (*na'*), which is translated "please" or "I beg you."[2] Rashi says *na'*

---

1. Wenham, *Genesis 16–50*, 104.
2. Hamilton, *Book of Genesis, Chapters 18–50*, 101.

is primarily an expression of entreaty,³ although in other instances Rashi explains *na'* as "now" (12:11; 19:2); here he says the meaning is "please" in order to avoid the idea that God caused Abraham to panic. In other words, by adding the word *na'*, God has given Abraham complete freedom of choice. Abarvanel, however, says that the word may be interpreted in two ways: "please take" or "take now." The meaning of "now" is the appropriate time to perform the task of taking his son and offering him as a sacrifice.

The identity of the sacrifice is described in ascending order to stress the severity of the sacrifice: "your son, your favored one, Isaac, whom you love" (22:2). This description from the general to the specific is like the first command Abraham received from God: "Go forth from your native land, and from your father's house, to the land that I will show you" (Gen 12:1). In both instances, the phrase "go forth" is used. The ascending order and similarity between the two calls was noted in the midrash:

> "And He said: Take, I pray Thee, Thy Son, etc. (22:2). Said He to him: 'Take, I Pray Thee—I beg thee—Thy Son.' 'Which son?' he asked. 'Thine Only Son,' replied He. 'But each is the only one of his mother?'—'Whom Thou Lovest.'—'Is there a limit to the affection?' 'Even Isaac,' said He. And why did he not reveal it to him without delay? In order to make him [Isaac] even more beloved in his eyes and reward him for every word spoken. This agrees with the dictum of R. Johanan, who said: *Get thee out of thy country* (Gen 12:1) means from thy province; *And from thy kindred* (ibid.) from the place where thou art settled; *And from thy father's house*—literally thy father's house. *Unto the land that I will show thee* (ibid). Why did He not reveal it to him there and then? In order to make it more beloved in his eyes and to reward him for every step."⁴

Abraham is told to take Isaac to the land of Moriah. The only other time that this place is mentioned is 2 Chronicles 3:1, which says, "Solomon began to build the House of the Lord in Jerusalem on Mount Moriah." This association was the source of the belief that Mt. Moriah was in Jerusalem.⁵ In the book of Jubilees we read: "And Abraham called that place 'The Lord hath seen,' so that it is said in the mount the Lord hath seen: that is Mount Zion" (18:13). Zion is referred to as "the mountain of the Lord" in some

---

3. *b. Sanh.* 89b; *Gen. Rab.* 55:7.
4. *Gen. Rab.* 55:7.
5. *Gen. Rab.* 55:7; Kalimi, "Land of Moriah," 345–62.

The Binding of Isaac

biblical passages.[6] Ramban points to the interpretation that equates Moriah with the Temple Mount in Jerusalem, although there was no temple during Abraham's time. This suggests that the usage of the name Moriah, in those days, was prophetically given. Among modern scholars, Noth dismisses the identification because "the original tradition of Abraham, which like that of Isaac, was native to the Negeb, did not extend further to the north at all,"[7] while according to Levenson, if Genesis 22:1–19 is a later tradition than most of Abraham and Isaac's tradition, then it is more likely that the story refers to a Judean cult site which became important in Israelite tradition only with the Davidic monarchy.[8]

There is no Mount Moriah, in Genesis 22. Genesis mentions the land of Moriah "on one of the mountains" (v. 2). In the ancient world it was believed that the gods lived on mountaintops. Hence, the Canaanites worshipped "on the high mountains" (Deut 12:2). God revealed himself to his people on Mount Sinai (Exod 19). It appears that a mountain was an appropriate place for meeting God, as mentioned in the following text: "And Abraham names the site the Lord will see, whence the present saying, 'On the mount of the Lord there is vision'" (v. 14).[9]

As for the name Moriah, different interpretations were offered by our sages, who explained why it is called Moriah:

> "One said: To the place whence instruction (*hora'ah*) went forth to the world. While the other explained it: To the place whence religious awe (*yirah*) went forth to the world. (Similarly, the word *aron* (the Ark). R. Ḥiyya and R. Jannai –one said: The place whence *orah* (light) goes forth to the world. . . . To the place where incense would be offered, as you read, *I will get me to the mountain of myrrh –Mor*."[10]

Rashi pointed out that God did not say to slaughter Isaac because it was never his intention that he should be slaughtered. Instead it says that God told him "bring him up to the mountain and prepare him as a burnt offering." Since Abraham complied with the test and brought Isaac up, God told him to bring his son back down (v. 12). According to Rashi, "The Holy One Blessed Be He causes the righteous to wonder, and afterwards

---

6. Isa 2:3; 30:29; Mic 4:2; Zech 8:3; Ps 24:3.
7. Noth, *History of Israel*, 126.
8. Levenson, *Death and Resurrection*, 121.
9. Wenham, *Genesis 16–50*, 106.
10. *Gen. Rab.* 55:7.

Isaac

He reveals to them. All this (is done) in order to increase their reward." Although this is a very interesting interpretation, we should point out that the verb "to bring up" is used in connection with sacrificial offerings (Lev 14:20; 17:8; Josh 22:23; Judg 6:26; 11:31; 1 Sam 13:9; Jer 14:12; Ezek 43:24). More importantly, Abraham understood it as an actual slaughter, otherwise it would not be a test.

Following God's command, Abraham rose early in the morning. The Bible does not say a word about Abraham's emotional state or his inner feelings. This is quite surprising, as the previous chapter—the story of the expulsion of Ishmael—says, "the matter distressed Abraham greatly" (22:11). The rabbis say that even though it was hard on him, Abraham did not delay. He woke up early in the morning and saddled the donkey instead of having the servants do it. All of this shows that he was zealously hastening to perform his religious duty, which is why it is customary to perform the circumcision early in the morning.[11] They also point out that the love of God causes one to ignore normal rules of personal conduct.[12]

We believe that Abraham wrestled with his own thoughts, thinking about God's command all night long, thus he probably did not sleep and got up early. His activities in the morning point to his psychological state. He saddled his ass, took the two servants and his son Isaac, and split the wood. It is strange that he cut the wood last as it makes more sense to do it first. This illogical order shows that he was preoccupied; he was not thinking straight. He was trying to conceal the true purpose of the journey. He did conceal it from Isaac. Furthermore, his wife Sarah is not mentioned at all in this chapter. According to Josephus, Abraham concealed it from his wife Sarah and everyone in his household out of fear that she might hinder him from doing God's service.[13] It is strange that Abraham had to saddle the ass and cut the wood; these were the servants' tasks. Abraham was a wealthy man with high social status; all of this normally had to be carried out by the servants. The servants do nothing in the whole story; they are simply there. This is not a coincidence; Abraham tries to occupy himself to divert his thoughts from God's command.[14] We can sense that Abraham struggles within himself; he was preoccupied, and so he could not focus. The impression is that Abraham tries to delay the binding by procrastinating. In verse

11. *b. Pes.* 4a.
12. *b. Sanh.* 105b.
13. Josephus, *Jewish Antiquities*, 1.12.2.
14. Mazor, "Genesis 22," 87.

6 we read: "And Abraham took the wood for burnt offerings and put it on his son Isaac. He himself took the firestone and the knife." The order of his acts is highly significant. Abraham taking the knife is suspended until the last moment, as if to say he was delaying and hoping for a miracle.

Early in the morning Abraham saddled his donkey. He took his two young men, his son Isaac, and the chopped wood for offering. Not clear is why he carried the wood for three days. It is possible that he thought that he would not find wood in the place he was ordered to go, or he took good quality wood from his house for fear that he would not find the right wood for altar offerings. This is in accordance with the writing of the Talmud: "And any piece of wood in which a worm was found was disqualified from being used upon the Altar."[15] In addition he took his two young men with him. According to Abarvanel, he did it without explaining the purpose of the journey so as to avoid any questions. Also, Rashi says: for a man of importance is not permitted to embark on a journey without two men accompanying him.

On the third day, Abraham saw the place from afar. In the Hebrew Bible three days signifies a period of time. Hence, on the third day Laban was told that Jacob escaped (Gen 31:22); Moses was instructed by God to go to pharaoh and to ask him to let the Israelites go for three days into the wilderness to make a sacrifice (Exod 3:18). The Israelites traveled in the wilderness of Shur for three days (15:22). By mentioning three days, the Bible stresses the fact that a period of time passed by. It comes to show us that Abraham had the time to think and reconsider his actions. If Abraham complied with God's request and acted at once we could say that he was in a state of shock, that he was too emotional. The three days gave Abraham the time to make a clearheaded decision and without hastiness. Indeed Rabbi Akiba says in the midrash: "He tested him unequivocally, that people might not say that He confused and perplexed him so that he did not know what to do."[16]

When Abraham saw the place from afar he told his servants to stay with the ass. Therefore, the question becomes: What did Abraham see? Furthermore, God said that he would show Abraham the place for offering. However, the text does not say that God actually did this. Nevertheless, Sforno (Obadiah ben Jacob, ca. 1470–ca. 1550) maintains that divine providence directed his gaze to that spot and he perceived it as the place.

15. b. Mid. 2:5.
16. Gen. Rab. 55:6.

According to the midrash, "He saw a cloud enveloping the mountain and said: It appears that is the place where the Holy One, blessed be He, told me to sacrifice my son."[17] The midrash explains the word מקום *makom*, "place," as a reference to God; thus, Abraham saw the glory of Shekhinah*a* as a manifestation of God's presence.[18] According to the literal interpretation, he saw the land of Moriah from afar, which was well known to him.

Abraham told the servants that he and the lad would go up there to worship and that they would return. By using the plural form he concealed the purpose of the journey from Isaac. Commentators tried to explain the patriarch's behavior of utterly lying. Benno Jacob says that, unknowingly, Abraham did speak the truth.[19] Dillmann says that it was an expression of "quiet hope that God may yet determine otherwise,"[20] while in Genesis Rabbah we read: "He thus informed him that he [Isaac] would return safely from Mount Moriah."[21] In other words God informed Abraham, by making him unintentionally prophesize, *and we will come back*. Hebrews 11:17–19 portrays Abraham's words as an example of the patriarch's faith that God was able to raise Isaac. No indication is given as to why Abraham wanted the servant out of his way. Several suggestions have been given, such as that God told him to leave them, or Abraham did not want them to see the sacrifice, but more likely he was afraid that they might interfere. It is noteworthy that Abraham refers here to his son Isaac as "the lad" rather than "my son." Thus, we can say that he has already given Isaac to God and, in a sense, Isaac is no longer Abraham's son.[22]

Abraham took the wood and put it on Isaac. It is Isaac who carries the instrument of his own destruction. As the midrash says, "like one who carries his stake on his shoulder."[23] The one to be executed carries his own stake, whereas Abraham carried the fire and the knife. The fire probably refers to firestone since it is unlikely that he carried fire for three days. As for the knife, the Bible uses the rare Hebrew מאכלת (*ma'akhelet*). This word is found in Judges 19:29 where it has the meaning of cutting up a human

---

17. *Gen. Rab.* 56:1.
18. PdRE ch. 31.
19. Jacob, *First Book of the Bible*, 144.
20. Dillmann, *Genesis*, 144.
21. *Gen. Rab.* 56:2.
22. Wenham, *Genesis 16–50*, 107.
23. *Gen. Rab.* 56:3.

The Binding of Isaac

body, and in Proverbs 30:14 where it refers to a sword.[24] What we have in the Genesis text is wordplay of the word knife *ma'akhelet*, and the word מלאך (*mal'akh*, angel): the angel who saved Isaac from the knife of death. Abraham laid the wood of burnt offering on Isaac, which is reminiscent of Abraham placing the bread and water on Hagar's shoulders. In both cases the patriarch is going to cut himself off from his own family.

According to the Bible "the two walked together" (v. 6), which implies complete harmony; Abraham knew what he was going to do—that is, to slay his son—and Isaac knew nothing. One was to slaughter and the other to be slaughtered. Still they went together in the same spirit. Until now Isaac did not know the purpose of the trip. The silence is broken when Isaac addresses his father and asks, "Where is the lamb for offering?" He noticed the fire and the wood, but the crucial element for the sacrifice was missing. In response, Abraham said that God will seek out for himself the lamb for the offering. In other words, we are preparing for the offering but God will choose the lamb. The phrase "and the two of them walked together" is repeated again in verse 8. It is mentioned after Abraham said that God himself will provide the sacrifice. This repetition was suspicious in the eyes of the interpreters. It was suggested that, at that moment, Isaac understood that he would be the lamb for the burnt offering. Indeed the midrash says: "God will provide Himself the lamb, O my son; and if not, Thou art for a burnt-offering, my son."[25] According to Rashi, even though Isaac understood that he was going to be slaughtered, they still walked forward with a common purpose.

Upon arriving at the place, Abraham built the altar. Previously, Abraham built altars as a result of God's promises (12:7, 8; 13:18); now he built an altar as a response to God's order which threatened those promises. It was not an ordinary altar, but *"the altar."* The usage of the definite article *"the altar"* may indicate an existing altar that was rebuilt by Abraham. This view is found in the midrashim. In Pirkei d'Rabbi Eliezer, this is the altar where Adam sacrificed, where Cain and Abel sacrificed, and where Noah and his sons sacrificed.[26] However, we should point out that the place was unknown to Abraham. The usage of the definite article came to stress and commemorate this place as *"the altar"* of the binding of Isaac.

The Bible describes the stoic regularity in which Abraham proceeded. First, he built the altar, then he arranged the wood, and then he tied his

---

24. Sarna, *JPS Torah Commentary: Genesis*, 152.
25. *Gen. Rab.* 56:4.
26. PdRE ch. 31.

Isaac

son. According to Abarbanel, this shows that Abraham acted with a clear mind—he was aware of what he was doing, he did not act in an impulsive manner. He bound Isaac and laid him on the altar. The Hebrew word עקד (*'kd*), "bound," is not found anywhere else in the Hebrew Bible. According to the Talmud, it means the tying of hands and feet.[27] Isaac's hands and feet were tied together behind him, and his neck was stretched backwards. The Jewish tradition named Genesis 22 the עקדה (Akedah) after the verb. Abraham's act of tying Isaac to the altar atop the wood is unusual. The explanation for this abnormality may lie in the fact that this is the only account of the procedure for human sacrifice.[28] When Abraham stretched his hand and took the knife to slaughter his son, the angel of the Lord called from heaven. Angels need to travel between heaven and earth, but here, because it was an urgent moment, the angel called from heaven. This call from heaven is reminiscent of the call the angel made to Hagar in 21:17. In other words, Abraham's two sons were saved by a call of an angel from heaven. The angel called Abraham's name in rapid succession—"Abraham, Abraham"—which expressed the urgency of the moment. According to Pesikta Rabbati:

> Abraham was hastening to cut Isaac's throat, and like a man crying out in sharp distress, the angel burst out at him: What are thou at? Abraham turned his face toward the angel. When the angel burst out: "What are thou at? Lay not thy hand upon the lad."[29]

The angel told Abraham not to harm his son. Ramban explains that Abraham's fear of God was still concealed; it had not yet emerged into actuality by means of a great deed. But now, with the attempted performance of this deed, it became known in deed and his merit became complete. The words "For now I know that you are a God-fearing man" troubled commentators. How could it say that he knew only now that Abraham feared him? Furthermore, there is a contradiction between "now" and "knew" which is in the past tense. Rashi resolved the difficulties by saying: "I have something with which to answer Satan and the non-Jewish nations who wonder what is the cause of My love for you. I have a justification that they see 'that you are God-fearing.'"

The text does not record a verbal response by Abraham to the angel's call nor Isaac's reaction to his release from the altar. What the text

---

27. *b. Shab.* 54a.
28. Levenson, *Death and Resurrection*, 135.
29. PR 40.

describes is how Abraham saw a ram caught in the thicket by its horn. The appearance of the ram was a total surprise to Abraham as the Hebrew word והנה *wehinnēh,* literally "and lo," suggests. Before, Isaac asked, "Where is the sheep?" (v. 7), and Abraham answered "God will see to the sheep for His burnt offering." Here God provided an animal, but a different one from what Abraham expected. According to Radak, he looked about to see if there was another ritually clean animal which he could offer instead of his son. Abraham was ordered to sacrifice his son, since this command was nullified, he needed to make a substitute.

Abraham named the place "The Lord will see." Naming a place was important in the ancient world. The place of theophany became a holy place and future generations venerated it. It turned into a cultic center where people would make sacrifices and pray to God. The name of the place reflects Abraham's reaction to his personal experience and is linked to verse 8. As Gunkle noticed, "Abraham gratefully remembers the words he spoke in extreme duress to his son (v. 8): "God will see it."[30] Similarly, Radak understood the name as an allusion to Abraham's prophetic assurance to Isaac: "God will seek out for himself the lamb for burnt offering" (v. 8). Von Rad believed that the narrative concluded with verse 14, comprised of God's appearance, the offering of the sacrifice, and the naming of the place. The second call by the angel in verse 15 is an addition to an ancient cult legend. It was added in order to link the narrative with the motif of "promise" which unites all of Abraham's narratives.[31] However, it is possible that the second call came because the angel's first address was interrupted by the sacrifice of the ram. After Abraham proved his obedience to God's will, all the previous promises needed to be reaffirmed. For the first time the promises are introduced by a solemn oath, with God swearing by his own being.[32] As Radak comments, it is an irrevocable oath: "Just as I am eternal, so is My oath eternal." The midrash raises the question: What was the need for this oath?

> He had begged Him: "Swear to me not to try me again henceforth, nor my son Isaac." R. Levi in the name of R. Ḥama b. R. Ḥanina gave another reason for this oath: He had begged: "Swear to me not to test me again henceforth."[33]

---

30. Gunkel, *Genesis*, 236.
31. Von Rad, *Genesis*, 242.
32. Sarna, *JPS Torah Commentary: Genesis*, 154.
33. Gen. Rab. 56:11.

Isaac

ISAAC IN LIGHT OF THE AKEDAH

The climax of the Isaac narrative is the story of his binding. Even in this story he plays a secondary role to his father Abraham, who is the main character. As a child he was submissive, which is evident from his silence at his sacrifice. He carries the wood that was supposed to be used for his own sacrifice and walks in silence at his father's side on the way to Mount Moriah. The only time that he speaks is when he asks about the sheep for the burnt offering. Abraham uttered an ambiguous response and still Isaac maintained his silence. Isaac accepted his father's response; he trusted his father. Alternatively, he may have sensed that he was the intended sacrificial lamb. If this was the case, it shows his total obedience to his father.[34] Abraham appears as the dominant father and Isaac as the archetypical submissive son. Abraham overshadows his timid son, Isaac, who displays no personality apart from his father. It appears that Isaac was a willing victim. There is no indication in the text that Isaac resisted his father or tried to flee. Abraham was an old man and Isaac was probably thirty-seven years old; he could have easily escaped.[35] Thus, Josephus in his writings observed:

> [Abraham tells Isaac that he is to be the sacrifice.] Isaac, however, since he was descended from such a father, could be no less noble of spirit [than Abraham], and received these words with delight. He said that he never would have been worthy of being born in the first place were he not now to carry out the decision of God and his father and submit himself to the will of both.[36]

A similar view is found in the writings of 1 Clement:

> "Why was our father Abraham blessed? Was it not because he acted righteously and truthfully through faith? Isaac knowing full well what was to happen was willingly led forth to be sacrificed."[37]

This shift from the passive Isaac to a willing victim is also found in the rabbinic writings. In Genesis Rabbah we read of a debate between Isaac and Ishmael:

---

34. Wenham, *Genesis 16–50*, 108.

35. According to *Gen. Rab.* 56:8, Isaac was twenty-six years old while, in a pre-rabbinic Jewish tradition, he was fifteen (Jub. 17:15–16).

36. Josephus, *Jewish Antiquities*, 1:232.

37. 1 Clem. 31:2–4.

Isaac and Ishmael were engaged in controversy: the latter argued, "I am more beloved than thou, because I was circumcised at the age of thirteen"; while the other retorted, "I am more beloved than thou, because I was circumcised at the eight days." Said Ishmael to him: "I am more beloved because I could have protested, yet did not." At that moment Isaac exclaimed: "O that God would appear to me and bid me cut off one of my limbs! then I would not refuse." Said God: Even if I bid thee sacrifice thyself, thou wilt not refuse.[38]

A later midrash Sifre Deut 32 from the end of the fourth century portrays Isaac as binding himself:

R. Meir says: Scripture says, *Thou shalt love the Lord, thy God, with all thy heart.* Love Him with all your heart, as did your father Abraham, of whom it is said, *But thou Israel, My servant, Jacob, whom I have chosen, the seed of Abraham My friend* (Isa 41:8). *And with all thy soul*, as did Isaac, who bound himself upon the altar, as it said, *And Abraham stretched forth his hand and took the knife to slay his son* (Gen 22:10).

Similarly, we find in Leviticus Rabbah: "Isaac fulfilled that which is written in the Torah, in that he cast himself before his father as a lamb that is to be sacrificed."[39] On the other hand, in Genesis Rabbah, we find that Isaac must be tied so he will not fall into temptation:

R. Isaac said: When Abraham wished to sacrifice his son Isaac, he said to him: 'Father I am a young man and am afraid that my body may tremble through fear of the knife and I will grieve thee, whereby the slaughter may be rendered unfit and this will not count as a real sacrifice; therefore bind me ever firmly.[40]

In another text, the *Biblical Antiquities* (of Pseudo-Philo, first century CE), we read that since Isaac was a willing victim he was announcing that his sacrifice would be more effective than the other sacrifices for future generations:[41]

And as he [Abraham] was setting out, he said to his son, "Behold now, my son, I am offering you as a burnt offering and I am returning you into the hand of Him who gave you to me." But the son

---

38. *Gen. Rab.* 55:4.
39. *Lev. Rab.* 2:10.
40. *Gen. Rab.* 56:8.
41. *LAB* 32:2–4.

said to the father, "Hear me, father. If [ordinarily] a lamb of the flocks is accepted as a sacrifice to the Lord with sweet savor, and if such flocks have been set aside for slaughter [in order to atone] for human iniquity, while man, on the contrary, has been designated to inherit this world–why should you be saying to me now, 'Come and inherit eternal life and time without measure'? Why if not that I was indeed born in this world *in order* to be offered as a sacrifice to Him who made me? Indeed, this [sacrifice] will be [the mark of] my blessedness over other men–for no such thing will ever be [again]–and in me the generation will be proclaimed and through me nations will understand how God made human soul worthy for sacrifice.

Christians saw in the binding of Isaac the foreshadowing of the crucifixion. In the Epistle of Barnabas (ca 70–132 CE), it was said:

"Whoever does not keep the fast shall surely die" was written, the Lord commanded it because he himself was planning to offer the vessel of his spirit as a sacrifice for our sins, in order that the type established by Isaac, who was offered upon the altar, might be fulfilled"[42]

The book of Romans says, "If God is for us, then who is against us? He who did not spare his own son but gave him up for us all, will he not also give us all things along with him?"[43]

Irenaeus, Bishop of Lugdunum, said that:

"Abraham, according to his faith, followed the commandment of the Word of God, and with a ready mind Abraham delivered up, as a sacrifice to God, his only-begotten and beloved son, in order that God also might be pleased to offer up for all his seed his own beloved and only-begotten Son, as a sacrifice for our redemption."[44]

According to the Christian theologian Augustine (354–430 CE),

"for this reason, even as the Lord carried his own cross, so Isaac himself also carried to the place of sacrifice the wood on which he too was to have been placed. Finally, since it was not fitting that Isaac should be slain, now after his father had been forbidden to strike him, who was that ram whose immolation completed the sacrifice by blood that was fraught with meaning? Note that when

42. Barn. 7:3.
43. Rom 8:31–32.
44. Irenaeus, *Against the Heresies*, 4.5.4.

The Binding of Isaac

Abraham saw the ram it was caught in a thicket by its horns. Who then was symbolized by the ram but Jesus, crowned with Jewish thorns before he was sacrificed?"[45]

After the binding, the text says that Abraham returned from Moriah, but there is no mention of Isaac. "Abraham then returned to his servant, and they departed together for Beer-sheba; and Abraham stayed in Beer-sheba" (Gen 22:19). It is possible that Isaac did not return with his father. The trauma of a near-death experience broke the bond between father and son; there was no longer trust between them. They never spoke again—each of them went his own way. Indeed, the rabbis asked: "And where was Isaac? R. Baḥya ben Asher (thirteenth century) said in the name of the Rabbis of the other place: He sent him to Shem to study Torah."[46] In Targum Pseudo-Jonathan we read that the angels took Isaac to the school house of Shem and he was there for three years. This explains the fact that he was thirty-seven years at the time of the Aqedah and forty when he returned from the school of Shem and married Rebekah.

THE PURPOSE OF THE STORY

It is not clear why God had to put Abraham through such an ordeal. God knows everything; so why is he asking Abraham to do such a cruel thing? According to Maimonides, "The sole object of all the trials mentioned in Scripture is to teach man what he ought to do or believe; so that the event which forms the actual trial is not the end desired; it is but an example for our instruction and guidance."[47] Maimonides says that God tested Abraham because he knew that he would pass the test. Abraham's faith would shine like a beacon and be a sign to the nations. The emphasis is not on Abraham's suffering but on his strength. According to Speiser, the object of the test "was to discover how firm the patriarch's faith was in the ultimate divine purpose."[48] The fact that this was a test was divulged to the reader at the beginning. This was done in order to remove any misunderstanding that God demands human sacrifice. Since the reader knows that God does not require a human sacrifice the main focus is Abraham. What is left for

---

45. Augustine, *City of God*, 16.32.
46. *Gen. Rab.* 56:11.
47. Maimonides, *Guide of the Perplexed*, 3:24.
48. Speiser, *Genesis*, 166.

the reader to see is whether Abraham will comply with God's request or not. God knew how Abraham would respond but wanted Abraham to discover his strength of faith. Abraham's passing the test serves as an example to the next generation of Israel. Abraham is the father of the faith who passed the test and trusted God, so likewise all devotees of Yahweh should do. The story stands in contrast to Abraham's lack of faith portrayed in stories such as 12:10–20 and chapter 16.

In the Rabbinic literature, this was the last of the ten trials to which Abraham was subjected.[49] According to Abarvanel, this is the only one of Abraham's ten trials that the Torah calls a test. In the other incidents, Abraham completed the trials. He indeed left his homeland, sent away Ishmael, and so on. Here, in our story, it remained nothing more than a test since God did not allow Abraham to slaughter his son. This was also the last theophany Abraham received from God.

Modern scholars maintain that the story was an etiological legend and that its purpose was to explain why the custom of sacrifice of a child at a certain place was substituted by the sacrifice of a ram.[50] It is a transitional story between human sacrifice and animal sacrifice. But this understanding of the story cannot be supported in light of the biblical tradition. Sacrifice is already mentioned in the story of Cain and Abel where animals and products of the soil constitute an offering (Gen 4:3). Noah, when he came out of the ark, sacrificed animals and birds (8:20). The substitution of a ram for Isaac was Abraham's own idea and was not ordained by God. Animal sacrifice was a custom that was practiced regularly in the ancient world since it was believed that the gods needed animal sacrifices to exist.

Human sacrifice, and especially child sacrifice, was widespread among the Canaanites, Phoenicians, Egyptians, and also among the Moabites and Ammonites. The Bible condemns this practice: "Do not allow any of your offspring to be offered up to Molech" (Lev 18; 21; 20:2; Deut 12:31). Molech is a deity that was worshipped by some of Israel's neighbors. According to

---

49. *'Avot* 5:3; There are several versions of what the test was. Following is the list of tests given by the Rambam: (i) Abraham exiled from his family and homeland, (ii) the hunger in Canaan after God had assured him that he would become a great nation there, (iii) the corruption in Egypt that resulted in the abduction of Sarah, (iv) the war with the four kings, (v) Abraham's marriage to Hagar after having despaired that Sarah would never give birth, (vi) the commandment of circumcision, (vii) Abimelech's abduction of Sarah, (viii) driving Hagar away after she had given birth, (ix) the very distasteful command to drive away Ishmael, and (x) the binding of Isaac on the altar.

50. Gunkel, *Genesis*, 239–40; Skinner, *Genesis*, 332.

The Binding of Isaac

2 Kings 23:10, it was King Josiah who destroyed a cultic site in the vicinity of Jerusalem where children had been sacrificed to Molech. This form of sacrifice was prevalent during the reign of Manasseh, King of Judah. In 2 Kings 16:3, we read that King Ahaz of Judah burned his own son in a fire. The Moabite king, Mesha, sacrificed his son during the battle on the field in order to achieve victory (2 Kgs 3:27). Jephthah sacrificed his daughter in fulfillment of a vow to get a military victory (Judg 11). Later we read of the denunciation of human sacrifice by the prophets Jeremiah and Ezekiel. The fact that the kings of Israel practiced human sacrifice and the prophets denounced it shows that human sacrifices still continued. Therefore, the story of the binding of Isaac was not a transitional story from human sacrifice to animal sacrifice. Nevertheless, one of its goals was to denounce human sacrifice.[51] In other words, human sacrifice is not the right way to worship God; thus, we read of the prohibition of it and its denunciation. Indeed, the prophet Micah mentioned the futility of child sacrifice: "With what shall I approach the Lord.... Shall I approach him with burnt offerings.... Shall I give my firstborn for my transgression, the fruit of my body for my sins?" (6:6–7).

Gunkel pointed to expressions such as *Adonai yireh* (14b), *Elohim yireh* (v. 8), and *vyirah vhineh 'ayil* (v. 13), and from this he concluded that the original name of the sanctuary was ירואל Jeruel. He identified the site with יריאל Jeriel that is mentioned in 2 Chronicles 20:16, which is near Tekoa. The substitution of Moriah for Jeruel/Jeriel was because the close similarity of the name of the cult site to Ariel, one of the names of Jerusalem (Isa 29:1–8). Thus, according to him, Genesis 22 was originally a legend of child sacrifice at Jeruel. It tells the reader that the deity wanted the firstborn son as a sacrifice, but explained how the deity accepted a goat as a substitute for the boy.[52] In other words, the basis of Genesis 22 was a local cult legend of this place. However, this is no more than philological speculation. This place is mentioned once in all of Scripture and there is no evidence that it ever served as a cult site. The story had to be more than an explanation of the name of a place or a protest against human sacrifice. The story as it appears has a deeper meaning.

Noth says that the story is a folk narrative which was passed orally. It was originally about a child that was symbolically offered on the altar but

---

51. Skinner, *Genesis*, 331–32.
52. Gunkel, *Genesis*, 238–39.

at the last moment was substituted by a ram.[53] Reading the story in Genesis shows that there are so many obscure details that the story cannot be analyzed historically with any certainty. Because Isaac plays such a passive role, the identification of the "son" with Isaac is late tradition, historically. Originally the story must have dealt with another figure. The merging of the southern wilderness Isaac tradition with the Abraham tradition occurred most likely in the context of the six-tribe confederacy of Hebron. In this manner the Isaac tradition was absorbed into the dominant Abraham tradition and consequently made Isaac the son of Abraham, their ancestral patron.[54] However, there is no support for his suggestion in the biblical text so this is purely guesswork.

In conclusion, the story of the binding of Isaac is not a transitional story between human sacrifice and animal sacrifice. Sacrificing animals is already mentioned before Abraham's time and human sacrifice lasted long after Abraham's time. What the story conveys is that human sacrifice is not the right way to worship. God knew that Abraham would pass the test. By Abraham passing the test it shows his obedience and love of God; it is a sign of strength for his faith. Abraham's love and trust in God serves as model to other nations. Abraham was tested here because from his first call in Haran, he was only rewarded, receiving promises of land and many descendants. Abraham is designated as the father of a new nation and as such he has to prove his worthiness to God. Therefore, through the whole episode the focus is on Abraham. Not surprisingly, Isaac is overshadowed by his father Abraham and is passive. In the midrashim he is portrayed as a willing victim who did not resist his father. Christians saw in the binding of Isaac the foreshadowing of the crucifixion. This passivity of Isaac will again be manifested in the story of his marriage to Rebekah, which will be the subject of our next chapter.

---

53. Noth, *History of Pentateuchal Traditions*, 114–15.
54. Ibid, 115n329.

3

A Wife for Isaac

FOLLOWING THE BINDING STORY of Isaac, the next episode where the patriarch appears is in the story of his marriage to Rebekah. As long as Isaac is not married, the promises that were given to his father, Abraham, for many descendants and the inheritance of the land remain unfulfilled. Isaac is the sole heir to the Abrahamic covenant; thus, the story of his marriage is significant. This story is found in chapter 24, which is the longest chapter in Genesis. It starts with Abraham's instructions to his servant to go to his birthplace to bring a wife for Isaac and ends with Isaac bringing Rebekah to his mother's tent. In this way the narrator creates a transition from Abraham to Isaac. Now it is Isaac and Rebekah who are the heirs of the promise. The story is one of the most delightful stories in the Old Testament. Scholars agree that as far as genre, it is a novelle, which is a short story with a single plot and few characters.[1] A large space is designated for speeches; this distinguishes it from a narrative, which mainly focuses on events and actions. The chapter can be divided into five parts:

1. Abraham commissions the servant (vv. 1–9).
2. The servant's prayer (vv. 10–14).
3. The encounter with Rebekah (vv. 15–27).
4. The betrothal (vv. 28–61).
5. Rebekah and Isaac (vv. 62–67).

1. Von Rad, *Genesis,* 253.

Isaac

From a geographical point of view, the scene is not limited to one place; the story has three settings, shifting from one region to another:

1. The Canaan context: Abraham sent the servant to bring a wife for Isaac from his family.
2. The Aram Naharaim setting: The arrangement for Rebekah's marriage.
3. Back to Canaan, where Isaac and Rebekah get married.[2]

By mentioning where the action took place and how long it lasted, starting in Canaan and ending in Canaan, the narrator creates a link between the beginning and ending of the story.

Some scholars suggest that because the chapter has so many similarities with the other parts of the book of Genesis that it comes from a later stage of the Genesis composition.[3] Hence, we examine the structure and the setting of this chapter. In what era was this story written? What kind of story is it? Why was the story formed and what does it try to convey? These questions and others will give us a better understanding of the personality of Isaac, who appears in this story as a secondary character.

ABRAHAM AND HIS SERVANT

Endogamy was practiced among the patriarchs, therefore Abraham sent his servant to Aram Naharaim to the city of Nahor, to bring back a wife for his son Isaac. Nahor, Abraham's brother, married his niece Milcah; Abraham married his half-sister Sarah; later, Jacob would marry Leah and Rachel, the daughters of his uncle Laban. Parents initiated marriages, selecting a wife for their sons. Hagar took a wife for her son Ishmael from Egypt; Abraham sent his servant to bring home a wife for Isaac. Later, Isaac would order Jacob to marry a wife from his family. After Shechem raped Dinah, he told his father, "Get me this girl as a wife" (Gen 34:4). Likewise, Samson tells his parents: "I noticed one of the Philistine women in Timnah; please get her for me as a wife" (Judg 14:2). This practice of the parents' involvement in the marriage of their children is practiced even today in certain societies. The purpose of endogamy was to preserve family ties by marrying within one's own group, such as a clan, tribe, or family.

---

2. Bar-Efrat, "Some Observations," 167.
3. Wenham, *Genesis 16–50*, 139.

To ensure that his wish would be fulfilled, Abraham asked his servant to swear to him that he would not take a wife for his son from the daughters of the Canaanites. This demand is found later in the biblical law (Exod 34:16; Num 25; Deut 7:3). The demand for an oath was due to Abraham's advanced age. It is not clear why Abraham asked his servant for an oath, when he could directly demand it from Isaac. This is probably because Isaac is not allowed to leave the promised land. The servant is asked to swear by "the Lord, the God of heaven and earth." It was suggested that this phrase is from a late period since "God of heaven" is found in postexilic literature as it is foreign to the patriarchal stories.[4] However, in Genesis the whole phrase is mentioned "the God of heaven and the God of earth" (v. 3). In verse 7, where the Hebrew manuscript lacks the phrase "the God of heavens," the LXX adds "and the God of earth."[5] In texts that are derived from the Persian period, only the expression "God of heaven" appears.[6] However a parallel is found in Genesis 14:22—"I swear to the Lord, God Most High, Creator of heaven and earth"—which is considered to be an old text. It was customary to call heaven and earth to witness the making of a covenant (Deut 30:19; Isa 1:2). This tradition existed before Old Testament times.[7] In addition, swearing by the genital organ is a very ancient custom.[8] As pointed out by Sarna, this may be a reference to circumcision. Holding the circumcised membrum is a reminder of the covenant with God and by this act, it calls upon God as the guarantor of the covenant.[9] Rashi, in his commentary on the verse, says that when one takes an oath he must place his hand on a sacred object such as the Torah, scroll, or phylacteries. Circumcision was the first precept given to Abraham which was accompanied with pain; this was valuable to him, so he asked his servant to take his oath upon it.

The servant had some doubt about his mission, therefore he asked Abraham, "What if the woman does not consent to follow me to this land, shall I then take your son back to the land from which you came" (v. 5)? He did not doubt that he would find a suitable wife for Isaac. However, he did

---

4. Wenham, *Genesis 16–50*, 384; Von Rad, *Genesis*, 250; Rofé, "Sippur, 'Erusei Rivqa," 42–67.

5. Andrews, "Yahweh the God of the Heavens," 45–47.

6. According to Rendsburg, the expression "God of heaven," which appears in Jonah 1:9, Ezra 1:2, Nehemiah 1:4, 1:5, 2:4, and 2:20, and 2 Chronicles 36:23, fall under the influence of Aramaic אלה שמיא ' *Ĭlōah' sᵉmayyā*. See Rendsburg, "Some False Leads," 25.

7. Hillers, *Treaty Curses and OT Prophets*, 4

8. Von Rad, *Genesis*, 249.

9. Sarna, *JPS Torah Commentary: Genesis*, 162.

recognize the possibility that the woman might be reluctant to leave her family for a strange, faraway land, and that she may refuse to separate from her family. Therefore, he asked whether Isaac could go to Haran. From the servant's question, we can also surmise that the servant assumes the likelihood of the patriarch not being alive at the end of his journey. Abraham's response (vv. 7–8) shows his absolute faith in God that he would secure the right wife for Isaac. These words are the last words of the patriarch. It shows his trust in God in contrast to Genesis 15:2 and 15:8. God, who took him from the house of his father to give him descendants and this land, would not want his son Isaac to return there. Isaac's presence in Canaan symbolized the fulfillment of posterity and national territory. Isaac had to stay in the land of Canaan.

There is a brief description of the preparation, departure, and arrival of the servant to his destination. The narrator describes the good-sized party that the servant took with him; ten camels and all the bounty of his master. These details are essential for the later development of the story. It will serve as a test for the bride-to-be and presents for her family to make an impression on them. The luxuries that the servant took with him were also part of the *mōhar*. No details are given about the journey to Aram-Naharaim, which took at least a month.[10] This lack of information is due to the simple fact that nothing important took place.

THE SERVANT AND REBEKAH AT THE WELL

Arriving in the evening at his destination the servant went to the well. In the ancient world, people would head to the public well in order to replenish their water supplies and to get some information about the town. It was in the evening when the townswomen came out to draw water for their families. According to Malbim (Meir Loeb ben Yehiel Michael, 1809–1879) the servant was not interested in a wealthy girl for Isaac. He desired someone modest that would go and draw the water herself. To insure the success of his mission, the servant uttered a short prayer for guidance. He asked God to arrange the situation so that it would work out in accordance with his requests. He asked that he would recognize Isaac's wife-to-be. Sforno (Obadiah ben Jacob, ca. 1470–ca.1550) pointed out that:

> He did not make this a sign whereby he might recognize Isaac's destined wife, because that would be divination; rather he prayed

10. Speiser, *Genesis*, 183.

that it might fall out so; and so, it was with Jonathan the son of Saul (1 Sam 14:8–12). As for the saying of our sages, *An omen which is not as that pronounced by Eliezer, Abraham's servant, or by Jonathan the son of Saul, is not considered a divination* (b.Ḥul. 95b), their intent and meaning is: if the individual says it not as a prayer, but as divination, i.e., 'If thus and thus happens then I shall do this,' then he is guilty of divination.

The servant's prayer was answered immediately. Rebekah, who was born to Bethuel, the son of Milcah, the wife of Abraham's brother Nahor, came out with a jar. The Bible furnishes this information because Nahor also had children from a concubine. However, the child of a chief wife enjoyed higher status. We are further told that she was a very beautiful virgin "whom no man had known" (Gen 24:16). The Hebrew word בתולה *bĕtûlâ* indicates "a girl of marriageable age."[11] It was interpreted midrashically that Rebekah coming to the well that day was unusual; it was the guiding hand of the divine providence that led her there on that particular day to meet Eliezer. It is also suggested that the phrase should have read "behold Rebekah came out" rather than "was going out." According to the Zohar, Rebekah was *an exception to the rule*, for everyone else in the city was wicked, and she alone was righteous.[12]

In his prayer, the servant set criteria for the ideal bride. The girl must be sociable to strangers, must demonstrate unusual kindness to the animals, and must be willing to give of herself to others. In other words, in responding to the servant's request, "Please, lower your jar that I may drink" (v. 14); her response would go beyond his request and she would offer all that is needed. Noteworthy is the fact that there were ten camels, each of which would need to drink twenty-five gallons of water to recapture the loss of water as a result of the journey. It takes a camel ten minutes to drink this amount of water.[13] Rebekah had to go down to the spring to fill her jar then come up, repeatedly going back and forth, which points to her hospitable and kind nature. The Bible described her action with speediness: "She quickly emptied her jar . . . and ran back to the well" (vv. 19–20) This reminds us of Abraham when he prepared a lavish feast for the angels who visited him. The Bible used the same verbs "hurry" and "run" (Gen 18:2–7). All this time the servant was waiting silently to find out whether Rebekah is

---

11. Wenham, "Betûlāh," 326–48; Schmitt, "Virgin," 853–54.
12. Matt, *Zohar*, 2.1.132a.
13. Sarna, *JPS Torah Commentary: Genesis*, 164.

to be the bride for Isaac. According to Rashi, he saw that his plan was nearly successful, but he was, as yet, unsure whether she was of Abraham's family or not, while Sforno says that the servant should have tried to stop her from exerting herself, but he remained silent because he realized that God might be showing him that his mission was successful.

Rebekah did not ask for any payment for her service, which shows that she was gracious and the right wife for Isaac. When Rebekah finished watering the camels, the servant gave her a gold ring weighing half a *shekel*, and two bracelets weighing ten gold *shekels*. It is only then that he asked for her name and whether he could stay at her father's house for the night. It appears that the servant believed that God intervened to show him Isaac's future wife; therefore, he gave her the gifts first and only then asked about her identity. While according to the Ramban this question of identity preceded the giving of the gifts, R' Bachya (ben Asher, thirteenth century) interpreted it as past-perfect and he had said before giving her the gift. Interestingly, she does not give her name but instead gives her lineage; she is the daughter of Bethuel who was one of the sons of Nahor and Milcah. Nahor was Abraham's brother, while Milcah was the daughter of his other brother Haran. It is not clear why she does not mention her mother's name, instead we read of her grandmother. It was Benno Jacob who pointed out the marriage of an uncle with an orphaned niece by which Nahor fulfilled his duty toward his dead brother, Haran.[14] Rebekah answered his second question about lodging. She told him there was plenty of straw to feed his camels and a place to stay for the night. The servant did not ask about feeding the animals, but she mentioned it, which points to her hospitality and generosity. It is at this point that the servant realized that the Lord made his journey successful so he bowed and prayed to God. He thanked God for guiding him to the house of Abraham's kinsman.

The servant meeting Rebekah at the well is similar to two other stories in the Hebrew Bible where the groom meets his wife-to-be. Jacob met Rachel at the well (Gen 29:10–11), and Moses met Ziporrah at the well (Exod 2:16–22). In these stories, we read of a stranger who arrives at a place and meets his bride at a well. The bride later informs her relatives of her meeting with the stranger. It is believed that these kinds of stories are based on matchmaking from that era. Meetings would take place next to a well since this was the place where young girls would gather. After the meeting between the two parties was established, it was brought to the family's

---

14. Jacob, *First Book of the Bible*, 158.

attention. The family would agree to the match and a banquet would follow. In our story it is not the groom who arrived at the well but the servant as the matchmaker. The three stories have tests; in our story, it is the qualities of the bride that are tested. On the other hand, in the Jacob and Moses stories, it is the groom who is tested for his physical strength and behavior toward the bride-to-be. Despite the similarities between these three stories there are a few differences.[15] In Genesis 24, the encounter at the well is by divine aid, in Genesis 29, it is by occasion, and in Exodus 2, it is the situation which provides the occasion for the meeting. In our story, Isaac did not come to the well, as did Jacob and Moses in the other episodes. The drawing of water was done by Rebekah versus the drawing of water by Jacob and Moses. These differences highlight the passivity of Isaac and the determination of Rebekah.[16]

THE SERVANT AT REBEKAH'S HOUSE

Rebekah runs to her family to tell them about the stranger she met at the well. The fact that she runs to her mother's household instead of that of her father is puzzling. This leads scholars to believe that Bethuel was dead. However, if Bethuel was not dead, we might say that the lineage was through the mother.[17] If Bethuel was dead, then Rebekah's brother Laban is the head of the family and in this capacity, he is the one who negotiates his sister's marriage.[18] In Hebrew the name Laban is the feminine form meaning "moon." This is consistent with our knowledge about Abraham's forefathers who were idol worshippers. Furthermore, the moon god Sin was worshipped in Haran.

Receiving the news about the stranger, Laban ran to the well to meet him. Laban showed signs of hospitality as his sister did, but his was motivated by greed. The first detail mentioned is that Laban noticed the ring and the bracelets his sister was wearing. This greed foreshadows his later dealings with Jacob. He greeted the strangers with the words "Come blessed of Yahweh" (Gen 24:31). The phrase is a courteous greeting since Laban does not know the identity of the stranger. He invites the stranger and his camels to his house, which he has already prepared in advance.

15. Aitken, "Wooing of Rebekah," 11.
16. Hamilton, *Book of Genesis, Chapters 18–50*, 148.
17. Jay, "Sacrifice, Descent and the Patriarchs," 61–62.
18. Gottwald, *Tribes of Yahweh*, 314.

Isaac

Entering the house, the servant insists on telling the purpose of his mission. Chapter 24, verses 34–49 are a repetition of verses 1–27, with some omissions and additions. It is a long speech as the servant recounts his whole experience. This is a typical feature of the Near Eastern tradition which has its origin in oral transmitted literature. The servant's aim is to assure Laban that the match is from God who answered his prayer. Without this repetition, the reader would not know how the servant convinced Rebekah's family to agree to the marriage of their daughter.

He starts by introducing himself as Abraham's servant, stressing Abraham's wealth "Yahweh has blessed my master abundantly so he has become wealthy" (v. 35). Then he proceeds to explain his presence in Aram-Naharaim, and that Abraham has a son. Abraham ordered him to go and find a bride for his son. Abraham sent him to "my country my clan" (v. 4). The servant changed it to, "Go to my father's house . . . take a wife for my son from my clan and my father's house" (v. 38). In other words, Abraham sent him to his own family. He stresses the kinship between Isaac and Rebekah. He repeats with a slight change, "What if the woman will not follow me" (v. 39)? It seems that it would be wiser not to repeat it. On the other hand, he omits Abraham's command that he did not permit Isaac to go to his homeland (v. 7). According to Abarbanel, this is because they might understand it as a critical comment on their homeland. In addition, he did not mention Abraham being led out of Aram-Naharim by Yahweh with the promise of the land of Canaan, in order to not hurt their feelings. Another departure from the original version that the servant did not use was the term "oath" (v. 8) Instead he uses the term "imprecation," which is an oath that has a curse attached to it. Ibn Ezra says that by doing so, he wanted to impress them with the seriousness of Abraham's intentions. He also added "*Yahweh, before whom I have walked*" and by doing so, he shifted the theme of Abraham's blessing to Abraham's behavior.

In retelling the meetings with Rebekah, he makes some slight changes. At first Rebekah is called נערה *naḥărâ* "maiden" (v. 16); here the servant calls her עלמה *'almâ* "young woman" (v. 43), which refers to a young woman in the prime of her youth, implying that she passed a very challenging test. To stress that he was led by God, he changes the verb קרה *qārâ* "grant me" (v. 12) to שלח *ṣālaḥ* (v. 42). He omits Rebekah's invitation for overnight lodging (v. 25). Most important is how he changes the order of his actions. In verses 22–23, he first places jewelry on Rebekah and then asks for her name. In retelling the story, he first asks Rebekah for her name and then he places the jewelry on her nose and wrists (v. 47). He changes the order in retelling the story because he said that he was told to go to his master's father's house. So how could he give the jewelry to the girl without asking her name first? He ends his story by mentioning God's providence guided him "on the right way" (v. 48). Now that the decision is in their hands will they do as God has done? Or they will go against God's will? In other words, he wants to know where he stands.

Bethuel and Laban respond to the servant's query. What is perplexing here is the mention of Bethuel. So far, the only person who is mentioned is Laban, and in the ensuing negotiations it is Laban and his mother who are involved (vv. 53, 55). Furthermore, the servant gave gifts to Laban and his mother, and no presents to Bethuel the father. Therefore, some suggest that the MT *and Bethuel* is a gloss or corruption of ובתו *ûbēṯô* "and his household."[19] Another view suggests that "he was under his wife's thumb just as Rebekah was later to "organize Isaac."[20]

In response, Laban and Bethuel said, "The matter was decreed by the Lord." This was evidence that the servant succeeded in his mission. The sages interpret this response as proof that God ordains a man's proper mate.[21] In addition, Laban and Bethuel said, "We can neither discourage nor encourage," which was understood to mean "anything at all."[22] This means that they accepted and agreed to the servant's request for Rebekah.[23] Clark points out that since Yahweh made his decision, Laban is no longer free to exercise his own decision.[24] It is from God that Rebekah should leave and marry Isaac. In other words, God's guiding hand is present throughout the whole episode. The servant's religiousness is again stressed, as after hearing the response he bows to the ground before Yahweh.

Since the family agreed to the match, it was customary to compensate the bride's family. The groom had to purchase the right to receive the bride in marriage, and then he brought the bride to his tent. Thus, Abraham's servant gave objects of silver, gold, and garments to Rebekah while he gave presents to her brother and mother. Two types of gifts are mentioned here, one to the bride and the other one to her family. The payment to

19. Speiser, *Genesis*, 181–82; Westermann, *Genesis 12–36*, 382.
20. Wenham, *Genesis 16–50*, 149.
21. *b. MK* 18b.
22. Honeyman, "Merismus in Biblical Hebrew," 14.
23. Westermann, *Genesis 12–36*, 389.
24. Clark, "Legal Background," 273.

the bride's family came to compensate for the loss of the bride's services and her potential offspring. The girl was a financial asset because she performed important economic functions in her father's house. She tended the flocks (Gen 29:6, 9) and went to the well and drew water (Gen 24:11–16) for the family. The gifts that were given to the bride's family are called מגדנת *migdanot*, which is equivalent to the Akkadian *biblum* ceremonial gifts.[25] The term *migdanot* is used in the Bible as royal gifts and listed with gold and silver objects (Ezra 1:6; 2 Chr 21:3). It appears that the gifts that were given to Laban and his mother were equal to the bridal price.[26] The bride-money was later transferred to the bride by her family.

After a night of rest, which was preceded by eating and drinking, the servant demanded, "Give me leave to go to my master" (v. 54). He was anxious to return home with the girl without any delay. He was probably afraid they might change their mind or that his master Abraham would not live to see his daughter-in-law. Rebekah's family, on the other hand, tried to stall; they wanted her to stay a few more "days or ten" (v. 55). According to Targum Onkelos. and Rashi, the plural "days" can mean "a year or ten months."[27] In the Talmud, we read that a year or ten months was the period given to a young bride to prepare for her marriage.[28] Therefore, Laban and his mother were making a reasonable and customary request. But the servant was afraid that they would break their commitment; therefore, he demanded to leave. According to Abarbanel, "Since everything has gone so smoothly and God guided my mission so speedily, it is obvious that he wished me to return to my master without delay."

The servant evidently did not convince Laban and his mother that he needed to leave at once with Rebekah. They suggested talking to Rebekah to ask her if she was willing to go immediately with the stranger. Speiser pointed out that according to the Nuzi contracts the woman's consent was requested as part of the marriage process.[29] Similarly, according

25. For Migdont see: Bar, "What did the Servant Give?," 565–72.

26. A different kind of substitute for bridal price is mentioned in the Jacob cycle. Jacob was a poor man when he arrived at the house of his uncle Laban. Therefore, he had to work for seven years in lieu of the bridal price. A similar situation is described in David's case. David had to replace the *mohar* with military service before his marriage to Saul's daughters (1 Sam 18:17–27). Later, he demanded that Michal be handed over to him since he acquired her as his wife for one hundred Philistinian foreskins.

27. On the meaning of the word "days," see North, "Four-Month Seasons," 446–48.

28. *b. Ket.* 57b.

29. Speiser, *Genesis*, 184–85.

to the Talmud, a girl should be given in marriage only with her consent.[30] Asking Rebekah for her consent was another ploy to delay the marriage. They were probably hoping that because of her attachment to her home she would ask for a delay. However, Rebekah replied, "I will" (v. 58).

Rebekah's answer left the family with no options so they sent her away with her nurse. This refers to her wet nurse, who raised her and looked after her from childhood. It is believed that it is Deborah (Gen 35:8). Before she left they blessed her thusly, "May you grow into thousands of myriads; May your offspring seize the gates of their foes" (24:60). It was suggested that the name "Rebekah" is wordplay on the root ברך bārak "to bless."[31] On the other hand, Gunkel suggests that the blessing of many offspring which uses the Hebrew word רבבה rĕbābāh is wordplay on רבקה ribqâ "Rebekah." The family gave Rebekah two blessings: one for many offspring and the second one for victory for her descendants over their enemies. The second part of the blessing, "May your offspring seize the gates of their foes" is like the blessing that Abraham received after the binding of Isaac (Gen 22:17). Westermann believes that the wish to increase in posterity has its origin in the wedding blessing (Ruth 4:11–12).[32] This section of the story ends with the departure of Rebekah, her maids, and the servant. The maids were part of her dowry, as later was the case with Rachel and Leah (29:24, 29). The servant achieved his mission; he did what Abraham told him to do. He succeeded in selecting a suitable wife for Isaac.

ISAAC AND REBEKAH

The last part of the story describes the meeting between Rebekah and Isaac. Isaac enters the scene for the first time (v. 62). The chapter starts with the formula "my master Abraham" and ends with "my master Isaac" (v. 65). Abraham is not mentioned, and according to Westermann "[i]t is presupposed that Abraham . . . is no longer alive."[33] The servant is reporting to Isaac not to Abraham. However, in the next chapter we discover that Abraham remarried and died at the age of 175 (Gen 25:7). Meanwhile, we are told that Isaac went from Beer-lahai-roi and settled in the area of the Negeb. He is no longer living with his father Abraham who lived at Hebron (23:2).

---

30. *b. Kid.* 41a.
31. Wenham, *Genesis 16–50*, 151.
32. Westermann, *Promises to the Fathers*, 153–55.
33. Westermann, *Genesis 12–36*, 391.

Isaac

In the evening Isaac went to the field, he went לשוח *lāśûaḥ*;³⁴ it is not clear what he was doing. Based on the root שוח *ś.v.ḥ*, which has the meaning of "to meditate, talk, complain," it was suggested that Isaac was praying; this is found in the targums (Onq., Neof., Ps.-J.) and rabbinic tradition (*Gen. Rab.* 60:14). Others interpreted, based on the Arabic *saḥa*, that he went "to roam, wander."³⁵ Rashbam explains that this refers to שיח *śiaḥ*, tree, and that he went to plant trees and watch the results of his labors. Speiser says that different interpretations are guesswork and Von Rad, commenting on "To meditate," says that it is guesswork and not even probable.³⁶

Isaac and Rebekah lifted their eyes at the same time: "he/she lifted up his/her eyes looked up" and "saw." Westerman says: "These two sentences reduce to minimum a meeting between two people so as to allow what is unspoken to speak all the more forcefully."³⁷ Isaac lifted his eyes and saw a caravan from across the fields. Rebekah raised her eyes and saw Isaac. How did she know that it was Isaac? They were travelling for a long period and saw many people during their journey. Therefore, it is possible that the servant probably spoke to her about Isaac during the journey, and from his description she assumed that it was him. Seeing that it was Isaac she jumped down from the camel and asked for the identity of the man who was walking in the field. The servant told her that it was his master, Isaac, so she took her veil and covered herself. She did it as an act of modesty. The veil was not worn by Israelite women permanently. However, it was customary for the bride that on her wedding night she was presented to her husband veiled (29:23–25).³⁸ Therefore, it was suggested that Rebekah kept her veil on until her wedding.³⁹

No conversation is recorded between Rebekah and Isaac. The servant reports to Isaac everything that he had done. The story ends with Isaac bringing Rebekah to his mother's tent. With this act, Rebekah became the next matriarch as the successor to Sarah. Isaac married her and loved her. To describe Isaac's actions, the biblical text uses the verb לקח *l-k-ḥ*, which means "to take."⁴⁰ The usage of the verb *l-k-ḥ* points to the early

---

34. For a summary of the various interpretations, see Greenspahn, *Hapax Legomena in Biblical Hebrew*, 160; Vall, "What Was Isaac Doing?," 513–23.
35. Simonis and Eichhorn, *Lexicon Manuale Hebraicum*, 955.
36. See: Speiser, *Genesis*, 185; Von Rad, *Genesis*, 254.
37. Westermann, *Genesis 12–36*, 390.
38. de Vaux, *Ancient Israel*, 33–34.
39. Wenham, *Genesis 16–50*, 152.
40. See also a priest may not marry לא יקחו (*lo yikḥu*) a woman defiled (Lev 21:7).

composition of the text; later the idiom for marriage was נשא *n-s-ʾ*, which is found in late biblical Hebrew (Ezra 10:44; 2 Chr 11:22; 13:21; 24:3) books written in the postexilic period. In the postbiblical tradition, it became the word that described marriage. According to the Ramban, Isaac was deeply grieved over the death of his mother and found no consolation until he married Rebekah. This is the second time that the Bible mentions love. The first time was at the binding of Isaac when it said that Abraham loved Isaac; it was the love of a father for his son (Gen 22:2). This is the first time in the Bible where we read of love between husband and wife. With the marriage of Isaac and Rebekah, Abraham's goal was achieved; the divine promises could be fulfilled. Isaac replaces his father Abraham, and Rebekah replaces Sarah. The promise of posterity and many descendants can now materialize.

THE PURPOSE OF THE STORY

Chapter 24 is the longest of the patriarchal narratives and has been called a novelette. It is a transitional story between the story of Abraham, which is near its completion, and the beginning of the Isaac story that will shortly unfold. The story starts with Abraham and ends with Isaac. The phrase "my master Abraham" gives way to "my master Isaac." The transition to Isaac and Rebekah as the successors of Abraham and Sarah as the heirs to the divine promises is manifested through the usage of key words and phrases.[41] Rebekah, like Abraham, had to leave her homeland. The patriarch obeying the divine call of "Go forth" is paralleled by Rebekah's willingness to go immediately. The blessing that Abraham received after the binding of Isaac, "Your descendants shall seize the gates of their foes" (22:17) is repeated to Rebekah (24:60). In addition, key words from Genesis 12:1–3 are repeated here, such as "native land" (vv. 4–7), "father's house" (vv. 3, 7, 8, 41), "to the land" (vv. 5, 7), "blessing" (vv. 1, 35), and "becoming great" (v. 35).

Wenham points out that not only are there many links between our story and the Abraham narrative, but also with the Jacob and the Joseph stories which follow.[42] Rebekah and Laban, who appear in chapter 24, are central figures in the Jacob stories (chs. 25–32), and the scene at the well (vv. 11–48) is parallel to the encounter between Jacob and Rachel at the well (29:2–14). There are links to the Joseph stories which are displayed

---

41. Sarna, *JPS Torah Commentary: Genesis*, 161
42. Wenham, *Genesis 16–50*, 137; von Rad, "Josephsgeschite und ältere Chokma," 120–27.

through specific verbal links. The subject of God's providence in human affairs is apparent in these stories.

The story in its current form is the fulfillment of the call-and-promise theme which is found in the Abrahamic narrative. The search for a wife and its outcome leads us back to that original call, a call that included blessings of many descendants and a blessing to those whom Abraham interacts with. Therefore, Rebekah's move from Aram to Canaan is destined by God. Rebekah is the next matriarch, and through her the line of Abraham will continue. Her departure is similar to the other matriarchs, as Sarah and later Jacob's wives, Leah and Rachel, also leave Aram upon the call of God. The wives of the patriarchs come from outside, which is in contrast to Ishmael and Esau, who married local women. Isaac and Jacob must marry within the family. Rebekah is the force behind Jacob and helps him to escape from his brother Esau. In Aram, he finds refuge in the house of his uncle Laban, who is first mentioned in our chapter. It is Leah and Rachel—Laban's daughters—whom Jacob marries that became the mothers of the Israelite tribes. Laban profits from his sister Rebekah and his two daughters; he receives the blessing from God. He receives the blessing that was promised to the nations through Abraham. The outcome of chapter 24 affirms the belief that the servant's successful mission to obtain a wife for Isaac is the result of God's providence. The ease with which the servant finds Rebekah, the consent of her family to the marriage proposal, and Rebekah's willingness to leave her home to go to a foreign land, all show that the mission was the result of divine providence.

The fact that it was God's guiding hand behind the scenes is recognized in the chapter (vv. 50–51). This is very similar to the book of Ruth where we read of the marriage between Ruth and Boaz.[43] Their marriage had important implications for the future of the Israelite nation. In Genesis 24, Isaac's marriage was to ensure the continuity of Abraham's seed and the nation of Israel. The outcome of Ruth's marriage would ultimately bring the birth of David the king of Israel. In Genesis, the servant went to Abraham's birthplace, to his homeland to find a wife for Isaac (24:4, 7). Meanwhile, in the book of Ruth, she leaves her father and mother and her birthplace to become Boaz's wife. In both stories, women leave their birthplace to fulfill a national goal. The events that take place in these stories are not a coincidence; there is a force which directs the ensuing events. The guiding hand of God is felt in the stories. In the meeting between Rebekah and the servant, the servant asked God הקרה נא *hakreh na'* "grant me good

---

43. Hals, *Theology of the Book of Ruth*, 44–47.

A Wife for Isaac

fortune" (v. 12). A similar language is employed in the book of Ruth ויקר מקרה *va-yikker mikreha* "and, as luck would have it, it was the piece of land belonging to Boaz" (Ruth 2:3). The root קרה *k.r.h* conveys happenchance, sometimes with theological implications of divine providence.[44] The reader is expected to recognize the hand of God at work. It was this happenchance that lead to the marriages of Isaac with Rebekah, and Ruth with Boaz. There are also similarities in the blessing. When the servant discovered the identity of the girl, he proclaimed: "*Blessed be the Lord*, the God of my master Abraham, who has not withheld his steadfast faithfulness from my master" (Gen 24:27). Similarly, when Naomi found out the identity of the man who owned the field to which Ruth went, Naomi said: "*Blessed be he of the Lord*, who has not failed in his kindness to the living or to the dead" (Ruth 2:20).

It was suggested that the story is a late composition. Theological dimensions were added to the story in order to create a link to the theme of promises, which is prevalent in the patriarchal narrative. In other words, there was a simple plot, and through the years details were added to it. Westermann believed that the story developed orally as a family narrative and was passed on as the different stories show. Genesis 24, in its current form, is a reworking of an older narrative with a new point of view, that of divine providence.[45] Van Seters also believes that the story is a late composition and assigned the chapter to J; he believes that it was composed in the sixth century.[46] Rofé, based on style content and linguistic features, suggested that it could not have been composed before 500 BCE. He points to religious belief about the importance of prayer, and not marrying Canaanites, which is one of the main features during the time of Ezra and Nehemiah.[47]

Conversely, examination of the Mesopotamian legal and social conditions attested in Nuzi tablets from the 2nd millennium BCE shows they reflect the same situation that is described in our chapter. The same marriage procedures that took place in Mesopotamia are found in our story. In marriage arrangements, it was the bride's brother who held important duties and powers with regards to his sisters.[48] As in our story, it is the brother who takes precedence over his father. In a marriage contract, which

---

44. Cohen Eskenazi and Frymer-Kensky, *Ruth*, 30.

45. Westermann, *Genesis 12–36*, 383.

46. Van Seters, *Abraham in History and Tradition*, 76–78.

47. Rofé "La composizione," 161–65; Rofé, "Sippur 'Erusei Rivqa (Bereshit 24)," 42–67.

48. Speiser, "Wife-Sister Motif," 62–82.

is referred to as "the sister manuscript," there is a clause where the young girl agrees to get married and in another case she and her brother agree to the marriage. Similarly in our story, Rebekah is referred to as "sister" (vv. 59–60) and she is also expected to give her consent to marry Isaac (v. 57). In addition, the parallel to the Jacob and Moses story of obtaining a wife in a foreign land shows that this custom was known in an earlier period.

As noted above, Chapter 24 shows dependence on the "theme call" of the Abrahamic narrative. The chapter contains many themes and motives which are reminiscent of the Abraham story, and as a result the chapter is dependent on previous events. As Matthews pointed out, "The chapter only works because its author counts on the reader's knowledge of the Abraham account and the Isaac and Jacob events re-imaging Abraham (21:2; 25:5; 26:12–13, 29; 29:1–14)."[49] Therefore, there is no need to date the story to a late period.

In conclusion, the story of acquiring a wife for Isaac serves as a bridge between Abraham and Jacob. It shows knowledge of and links to previous chapters in Genesis which includes the call of Abraham and the birth of Isaac. The genealogical link between Abraham and Isaac and the marriage of Isaac to Rebekah, the sister of Laban, presupposes the Jacob tradition (who marries the daughters of Laban). Indeed, there are many links to the Jacob story which follows it. The story is a fulfillment of the theme of "call and promise" which is found in the Abrahamic narrative. By taking Rebekah as a wife, Isaac becomes the sole heir to the Abrahamic covenant. Now the promises for many descendants and the inheritance of the land can be fulfilled. The outcome of chapter 24 affirms the belief that the successful mission of the servant is the result of God's providence. God's guiding hand behind the scenes is recognized in the chapter. The daily life of the patriarchs in ancient times matches those we read about in Mesopotamian legal and social traditions. There is no need to assign the story to a later period. Only a few verses describe Isaac's meeting with Rebekah and their marriage. Unlike Jacob and Moses, who met their brides at the well, it is the servant who meets Rebekah at the well. Isaac stayed at home. As in the story of the Akeda, Isaac appears as a passive person and a secondary character. Continuing with the theme of daily life, we will further examine the religious practices in the Isaac stories to see if indeed they reflect an earlier period.

---

49. Mathews, *Genesis 11:27–50:26*, 324.

4

The Religious Customs in Isaac's Stories

THE BOOK OF GENESIS has neither laws nor moral responsibilities. God gave only promises of nationhood and posterity to the patriarchs. Not surprisingly, some scholars claim there is no such thing as a patriarchal period or patriarchal religion.[1] Scholars maintain that these stories in Genesis are late retrojections composed during the monarchial period. The rabbis were also aware of the lack of moral responsibility and lack of law. However, they solved these difficulties by claiming the existence of a divine covenant with the whole human race. According to them, God made a covenant with Adam and Noah. This came to be known as the Noachian commandments. Nevertheless, examination of the book of Genesis shows that some religious customs and practices were already described in the book of Genesis, such as building altars, offering sacrifices, setting up pillars, planting sacred trees, praying, blessing, and circumcising. In an attempt to reconstruct the religious customs of the patriarchs and assign a precise date to the stories, scholars used extrabiblical sources. In spite of using similar data, they arrived at contrasting conclusions. Evidently, this kind of methodology had some flaws and did not offer an adequate solution.[2] One of the main problems is the fact that some of the religious practices and social customs in

---

1. Wellhausen, *Prolegomena to the History of Israel*, 318–19; Hoftijzer, *Die Verheissungen*, 6–30; Van Seters, *Abraham in History and Tradition*, 220–33.

2. Talmon, "'Comparative Method,'" 320–56; Warner, "Patriarchs and Extra-Biblical Sources," 50–61; Millard, "Methods of Studying," 35–51; Luke, "Abraham and the Iron Age," 35–47; Miller, "Patriarchs and the Extra-biblical Sources," 62–66.

the book of Genesis remained unchanged for centuries.[3] This, in turn, led scholars to reevaluate their thinking and methodology. Therefore, in order to identify the religious customs and practices of the patriarch Isaac, we will use a diachronic approach and examine the biblical text as it appears. In other words, we will identify the patriarch's historical beliefs by examining the different religious customs described in the book of Genesis that relate to Isaac. In addition, we will compare the customs to later periods in the biblical narrative. This in turn will help us to see if indeed the religious customs of the patriarch Isaac were authentic presentations of his faith during his time, or a representation of the later monarchial period.

ALTARS

Genesis mentions the building of altars quite often. The patriarchs built new altars and afterward they reused the ones they built. Following God's theophany at the terebinth of Moreh, Abraham built an altar as a way of showing gratitude for the promise of the land (Gen 12:7). Abraham built a second altar between Beth El and Ai, where he invoked the Lord by name (12:8). Returning from Egypt, he stopped at the same altar and invoked the name of God (13:4). A third altar is mentioned in Genesis 13:18, where Abraham, who lived by the terebinths of Mamre in Hebron, built an altar there unto the Lord. There is still another instance of Abraham building an altar in the story of the binding of Isaac. However, this altar was a different one; here he built an altar as a result of God's request to sacrifice Isaac. This fact is more significant because this is the only time that the patriarch made a sacrifice. Abraham built altars before, but there was no mention of sacrifice. It has been suggested that Abraham's altars were already sacred places.[4] This assumption was based on the use of the phrases "the place," "the Oak of Moreh," and "the Oaks of Mamre." In other words, this is a testimony to a primitive religion, animistic in its nature. However, "the place" does not always refer to a holy site.

Like his father Abraham, Isaac also built an altar to God and invokes God's name after receiving a theophany at Beer-sheba (26:25). Isaac received blessings on account of his father, therefore he was the heir of the blessing. According to Abrabanel, he built an altar to acknowledge God's beneficence and express gratitude for the prophecy God had just given him.

---

3. Freedman, "Chronology of Israel," 205; Selman, "Comparative Customs," 125–26.
4. Skinner, *Genesis*, 246; Westermann, *Genesis 12–36*, 153–54.

The Religious Customs in Isaac's Stories

The message from God included the promise of blessing with the promise of many descendants. It was "the God of the fathers" who appeared to Isaac. This is the first time that the epithet "God of your father," is used. The patriarch transformed the place into a cultic site where he invoked the Lord by name. It became a place of worship to commune with God. For the history of the cult, the Isaac tradition was bound to Beer-sheba. It is noteworthy that after God's earlier revelation in verse 3, Isaac did not build an altar. This was because Isaac lived in Gerar at the time, a land that did not belong to him. He probably was afraid to make public that he had been promised the land of his neighbors. In the second theophany the blessing was more general, therefore he did not have a fear of publicizing it. Following the building of the altar, he pitched his tent there, which implies that he established his dwelling place in that locality.

Later, Jacob would stop at the same site in Beer-sheba on his way to Egypt and use the same altar that his father Isaac previously built (46:1). It is possible that building an altar at Beer-sheba also served as a claim to the land of Israel since Beer-sheba was on the border of southern Israel. In addition, because the three patriarchs were connected to the sanctuary in Beer-sheba, it legitimized the sanctuary in later Israel. However, in the book of Amos we read that people stopped to receive oracles there (5:5; 8:14).[5]

The building of the altars was spontaneous; there are only two occasions where God instructed the patriarchs to build an altar (Gen 22:2; 35:1). The altars were a place to commune with God, therefore the patriarchs invoked God's name. The altars were built on the occasion of the epiphanies, not for sacrifice, but as enduring signs. They served as a sign of gratitude for God's promises. Segal explained the building of altars as the attachment of spiritual context to the place. Accordingly, the patriarchs built altars where they prayed to God but removed the pagan element, which was symbolized by the sacrifice.[6] The custom of the naming of altars or invoking God's name continued with Moses (Exod 17:15) and Gideon (Judg 6:24) but is not mentioned afterward. Only in one instance, the binding of Isaac, did Abraham make a sacrifice on an altar that he built (Gen 22:13). Not surprisingly, the patriarchs did not have priests. Priests would appear in Israel only after the Exodus, with the dedication of Aaron and his sons by Moses (Exod 28–29; Lev 8–10). Before the existence of priesthood, it was the head of the family who brought sacrifices and blessed the members of his family

---

5. Skinner, *Genesis*, 327.
6. Segal, "Religion of Israel before Sinai," 220–21.

(Gen 28:1–4; 48:9–20; 49:3–28). In the book of Exodus, the firstborn lead the community (Exod 22:28). In Exodus 24:5, they are referred to as the "young men of the people of Israel." However, they lost their important role after the story of the golden calf (34:26; Num 8:2–26). This change is echoed in Numbers 8:18: "Now I take the Levites instead of every firstborn of the Israelite."

SACRIFICE

The first mention of the patriarchs offering a sacrifice appears in the story of the binding of Isaac. Accordingly, Abraham took the ram and offered it up as a burnt offering in place of his son. As mentioned before, some suggest that the story of the binding of Isaac is a polemic against human sacrifice. The binding of Isaac is a transitional story from human sacrifice to animal sacrifice. However, examination of the biblical narrative does not support this view. Human sacrifice did not end with the binding of Isaac. On the contrary, we still read about it in the Hebrew Bible. The story had a didactic purpose to show Abraham's love and devotion to God. The sacrifice, which is described in the binding of Isaac, is typical to the patriarchal narrative. Neither a priest nor an established cult is involved. This matter is between the patriarch and God. It is different from later periods where organized sacrifice was offered during festivals and public occasions. The sacrifices functioned as a removal of sin and healing, neither of which are mentioned here.

PRAYERS

Prayers are mentioned several times in Genesis. The first time that prayer is mentioned is in Abimelech's dream. God told Abimelech that Abraham would intercede on his behalf and pray for him (Gen 20:7). In verse 17, Abraham prays to God and God heals Abimelech, his wife, and his slave girls. The prayer is mentioned here but the content of the prayer is not recorded. It was common for people to pray for one another. Later, Moses prayed for his sister Miriam (Num 12:13). Job prayed to God for his three friends (Job 42:8). This was also common in the ancient Near East where kings prayed for the healing of people and to avert divine judgment. A good example is Mursilis, who prayed to remove the plague that had affected his kingdom since the days of his father, Suppiluliumas I.[7]

In Genesis 24:12–14, when Abraham's servant was sent to Mesopotamia to bring a wife for Isaac, he prays for guidance. This is the first occurrence of a prayer for guidance. The servant starts his prayer with an appeal to God to "keep faith with my master Abraham." Then he requests a sign from God when he says, "grant me good fortune this day" (v. 12). He wants a sign on the same day. This is the first passage in the Hebrew Bible where God answers a prayer on the same day that it was prayed.[8] Recognizing that his prayer was answered, the servant bowed to the Lord, thanking God in a prayer (24:26–27). The action and the prayer in verses 26–27 are parallel to the prayer at the arrival at the well. The prayer itself is simple and starts with praise to God: "Blessed be the Lord," and is expanded to: "The God of my master Abraham, who has not withheld his steadfast faithfulness from my master." According to Towner, it is a spontaneous, noncultic blessing of Yahweh.[9] He believes that the usage of the formula, "Blessed be YHWH," was used in conversation between people, and it was uttered for the benefit of the listener.[10] Therefore, the servant was praying in the presence of the girl, and in the following verse may even be addressing her: "For I have been guided on my errand by the Lord, to the house of my master's kinsmen" (v. 27). No intermediaries are involved in the servant's prayer; it is a direct call for God's help. It was followed by a "thanks prayer" to God. The prayers were natural, spontaneous expressions of God's close relationship with his people.

Isaac's plea to God on behalf of his barren wife is also a form of prayer (25:21). God responded to his plea, so Rebekah conceived. Isaac, as the head of the family, was interceding on behalf of his wife. The Bible uses the verb עָתַר ʿātar to describe Isaac's praying. The meaning of the root is "pray, supplicate always to God."[11] The same verb is used later to describe Manoah, who turned to God after learning about the birth of his son. The root is often used in the account of the plagues in Exodus. Pharaoh entreated Moses to pray for him so the plague would disappear each time.[12]

---

7. Goetze, "Plague Prayers of Mursilis¹," 394–96.
8. Hamilton, *Book of Genesis, Chapters 18–50*, 145.
9. Towner, "'Blessed be Yahweh,'" 388–89.
10. Ibid., 389
11. BDB, 801; for a general study, see Gerstenberger, "עָתַר ʿātar; עָתָר ʿātār," 458–60.
12. Exod 8:4, 5, 24, 25, 26; 9:28; 10:17.

According to the Hebrew Bible, Rebekah experienced a difficult pregnancy, so she went to seek divine guidance. Rebekah's inquiry of the Lord can also be seen as a form of prayer. The Hebrew text uses the word דרש *dārash* "inquire," which has the meaning of "to consult an oracle, to inquire of Yahweh."[13] Elsewhere this involves going to a sanctuary or consulting a prophet. However, no information is given about the place of inquiry. Rebekah lived at Beer-lahai-roi, the place where Hagar received a theophany, which might have influenced Rebekah to go to the same site. The text tells us that Rebekah went to inquire of the Lord. The usage of the divine name "Yahweh" is not accidental; due to Rebekah's background she previously belonged to a family of idol worshipers. Therefore, the usage of the divine name Yahweh came to dissociate her action from the pagan cult. The result is a prophetic oracular in which Rebekah is informed that she is carrying twins; each will be a father of a nation; one nation will be stronger than the other; and the older will be a slave of the younger (Gen 25:23).

When Abraham worshipped, he invoked the name of God (Gen 12:8; 13:4; 21:33). The same act is mentioned with Isaac: "So he built an altar there and invoked the Lord by name" (26:25). The calling of the name is an act of worship. This invocation relates to the ancient Near Eastern notion of a connection between a person and their name. But the connection is not just lexical; it is symphonic since the way a name is pronounced has mystical implications on the meaning of that name. In the book of Genesis there is no suggestion that this form of prayer received a response from God. However, the form "call upon the name of the name of Yahweh" is found outside the Pentateuch only when an answer from the deity was expected (1 Kgs 18:24; 2 Kgs 5:11; Ps 116:14; Isa 64:6; Lam 3:55; Joel 3:5; Zech 13:9), or it is used doxologically (Ps 80:19; 105:1; 116:13, 17; Isa 12:4; Zeph 3:9).[14] We can see that prayers in the book of Genesis were a spontaneous outpouring of the heart. They were individual and tailored for the specific occasion. They were not connected to a specific site or a cult.

SWEARING

Swearing is another religious act mentioned in Genesis. In Abraham's pact with Abimelech, the king asked Abraham to swear to him. In addition,

13. Judg 6:29; 1 Sam 9:9; 1 Kgs 14:5; 22:5, 8; 2 Kgs 1:2; 3:11; 8:8; 22:13, 18; 1 Chr 34:21, 26; Isa 19:3; Jer 21:2; 37:7; Ezek 14:3, 7.
14. Hamilton, *Book of Genesis Chapters 18–50*, 378.

The Religious Customs in Isaac's Stories

Abimelech asked Abraham not to deal falsely with him or with his posterity (Gen 21:23).[15] Similarly, Isaac and Abimelech made a pact (26:31). Abimelech, his councilor Ahuzzah, and Phicol, chief of his troops, initiated the pact; they asked Isaac for a sworn treaty. A curse was attached to the treaty that was sealed by an oath. Isaac accused the king and his officers of hating him. He could not understand why they came to him since they had already expelled him from their territory. But as Abarbanel noted, it was the same Philistine king, or his father, that came to Abraham and made a treaty with him that was supposed to last for generations. Instead the king did not keep up with the covenant and his servants stopped up Isaac's well. That is why Isaac reacted in a negative way to their proposal. He realized that a pact with the Philistines was useless. The act of swearing gave the treaty its authoritative stamp. Abimelech demanded a "sworn oath" אלה (*ālâ*) between himself and Isaac in addition to a treaty ברית *berît*. This was followed later by the verb שבע *šāba'* "to swear." McCarthy proposes that the occurrence of this verb after *'ālâ* אלה and ברית *berît* "serves to affirm and record the fact that a covenant has been completed. It sums up the result of the action."[16]

Although not mentioned in the text, most probably the act of swearing was accompanied by lifting up the hands. Even today this tradition can be seen in customs such as raising one hand, while the other rests on the Bible, before testifying in a judicial court.[17] Later, the act included the holding of a Torah scroll, phylacteries, or a Bible. Abraham's servant, before he was sent on his mission to bring Isaac a wife, swears to Abraham by the Lord, the God of heaven and earth (24:3). It has been suggested that this expression is a Hebrew adaptation of an oath formula in which the gods of heaven and earth are summoned to witness an oath.[18] It also might be because the mission involves travel to a distant land that the servant invokes God's universal sovereignty. In addition, the servant puts his hands under Abraham's thigh, which is a euphemism for touching the genitalia. According to Vawter, we have here an ancient ceremony, "which reverenced the organ of the generation as the seat of life and symbol of sacredness: the same mentality

---

15. The Hebrew term "deal falsely" is found in the eighth-century-BCE Sefire treaty, meaning to be guilty of a breach of contractual commitment (Fitzmyer, *Aramaic Inscription of Sefire*, 107).

16. McCarthy, "Covenant-Relationship," 58.

17. Exod 6:8; Num 14:30; Deut 32:40; Ezek 20:23.

18. Andrews, "Yahweh the God of the Heavens," 45–47.

that found expression in phallic worship and fertility ritual."[19] The touching of the circumcised membrum is a reminder of the covenant with God, and by that act it calls upon God as the guarantor of the covenant.

BLESSING

The most common Hebrew word for "blessing" is ברכה *bĕrākâ*. It was believed that there is power in spoken words. Two major types of blessing are found in the Hebrew Bible: the pronouncement of the blessing and requests of blessings. When God does the blessing it is a decree, and when man does the blessing the source of power is the deity. The first occurrence of a blessing is found in Genesis 1:22, when God blessed the sea creatures and birds to be fruitful and multiply in the seas and the earth. Similarly, God blessed Adam and Eve and told them to be fertile and increase and to have dominion over creation (1:28). When God told Abraham to go to the land of Canaan he blessed him and promised to make his name great. In addition, Abraham would be a blessing to those who blessed him, so they too would enjoy God's blessing. Following the binding of Isaac, God again blessed Abraham as a reward for his devotion and obedience. God blessed him with posterity and victory over his foe.

God is not the only one who makes the blessing. Rebekah, before her departure to the land of Canaan, received a blessing from her family:

> O sister!
> May you grow
> Into thousands of myriads;
> My your offspring seize
> The gates of their foes (Gen 24:60)

The blessing contains posterity and security. What is interesting is that she received the same blessing that God gave Abraham following the binding of Isaac: "I will greatly increase your offspring" (22:17). In other words, her marriage is preordained and the divine promises are to come through her. In addition, her family wished that her offspring would always be victorious in battle. The blessing that Rebekah received, is used today at the veiling of the bride which takes place before the Jewish wedding ceremony.

---

19. Vawter, *On Genesis*, 267.

The Religious Customs in Isaac's Stories

The Bible does not mention that Abraham blessed his son Isaac. Targum Pseudo-Jonathan adds that Abraham refused to bless Isaac for fear that Ishmael might hate Isaac as happens later with Esau/Jacob. In the midrash, on the other hand, we read: "If I bless Isaac the children of Ishmael and of Keturah are included; while if I do not bless the children of Ishmael and of Keturah, how can I bless Isaac?"[20] So instead of Abraham's blessing, the Bible tells us that it was God who blessed Isaac (Gen 25:11). By mentioning it, the narrator confirms the transition of the divine blessing from Abraham to Isaac in fulfillment of the promise of 17:21: "But my covenant I will maintain with Isaac, whom Sarah shall bear to you at this season next year."

In contrast to Abraham, the inherited blessing is found in the Isaac and Jacob stories. Isaac is the first patriarch who blessed his sons. It was in his old age, on his deathbed, that Isaac decided to pass the blessing to his older son. He asked his son to go out into the field and hunt for him. By asking Esau to hunt for him, Isaac wanted Esau to receive the blessing by performing the later commandment of honoring his father. According to the sages, the prophetic spirit can rest only on one who is in the state of joy.[21] The repeated mention of preparing a meal suggests that eating a meal was part of the ritual of blessing. Isaac's request was not unusual as the Ugaritic text describes, for example, El taking "a cup in one hand, flagon in the other" and then blessing his servant.[22] When Isaac is blessing his sons, the source of the blessing is God. Isaac summons from the depth of his soul all the strength to aid him in order to invoke God's blessing on his son. His blessing has the power, due to his close relationship to God and of being the patriarch.

CIRCUMCISION

An important institution in the Jewish religion is the practice of circumcision.[23] This custom is first mentioned in Genesis 17:9–14. It serves as a sign of an eternal covenant between God and his people, like the rainbow and the Sabbath. In Exodus 4:24–26, circumcision comes to protect the person from the anger of God. The usage of a flint blade knife for circumcision points to the antiquity of this custom (Exod 4:25; Josh 5:2), since this

20. *Gen. Rab.* 61:6.
21. *b. Shab.* 30b.
22. Pardee, "Emendation in the Ugaritic Aqht Text," 53–56.
23. For general study on circumcision, see Morgenstern, "'Bloody Husband,'" 35–70; Morgenstern, *Rites of Birth, Marriage, Death*, 48–66; Hall, "Circumcision," 1025–31.

type of knife is from the Bronze Age. Abraham did not start the practice of circumcision because he knew what to do. Not surprisingly, the rabbinic legend suggests that it was known before.[24] In the book of Genesis, all the descendants of Abraham are circumcised: Isaac, Ishmael, and the sons of Keturah. Abraham was ninety-nine years old when he circumcised the flesh of his foreskin, and his son Ishmael was thirteen years old. Abraham also circumcised all his household; this included two groups of slaves. In contrast, Isaac was the first person circumcised when he was eight days old in accordance with the command in 17:12: "eight days old." This underscored his role as the true heir to the Abrahamic covenant. Abrabanel suggests that the phrase *at the age eight days* speaks of not only the time of circumcision, but also the time that Abraham named his son. Ramban, on the other hand, suggests that Abraham named Isaac on the day he was born because the name had been commanded by God (17:19). The sages derive from the word *him* that only the father is obligated to perform the rite of circumcision and not the mother.[25]

It is only with the end of the patriarchal period that the circumcision becomes a mark of ethnic difference. Indeed, the Hebrew Bible uses a negative tone when speaking of uncircumcised people. According to the Bible, the uncircumcised people included the Shechemites (Gen 34) and the Philistines. During the wars with the Philistines, the word "uncircumcised" became a term for the enemy (1 Sam 14:6; 17:26, 36; 31:4).[26] In the books of Isaiah and Ezekiel, the lack of circumcision is identified with cultic impurity (Ezek 44:7, 9; Isa 52:1; Exod 12:48). The prophet Ezekiel threatens the Phoenicians (Ezek 28:10) and Egyptians (31:18; 32:17–32) with lying among the uncircumcised in their death, as well as those slain by the sword, obtaining a special place in the underworld.

Circumcision is also mentioned in extrabiblical sources. According to Herodotus, Egyptians practiced circumcision "for the sake of cleanliness, considering it better to be clean than comely."[27] A stela from Naga ed-Der in Middle Egypt from 23 BCE gives us a report of a mass circumcision of one hundred and twenty men. A tomb relief from Saqqara from 2350 BCE depicts an operation on a boy. However, it is not clear if this practice of circumcision was widespread or restricted to a certain class. It is also

---

24. *Gen. Rab.* 42:8.
25. *b. Kid.* 29a.
26. For the term "uncircumcised," see Mayer, "עָרֵל 'āral," 359–61.
27. Herodotus, *Histories*, 2.37.

unknown if it was obligatory or voluntary. Circumcision among the Canaanites is found in the writings of Philo of Byblos: "At the occurrence of a fatal plague, Kronos immolated his only son to his father Ouranos, and circumcised himself, forcing the allies who were with him to do the same."[28] The Hebrews probably adopted the practice of circumcision as they moved into Canaan (Gen 17; Josh 5:2–9).[29] Israel's neighbors stopped the practice of circumcision during the Second Temple period as a result of Persian and Greek cultural influences. From that period onward, circumcision became a sign of recognition for Jews and converts to Judaism.

In conclusion, examination of the Isaac narrative shows no regular patterns of worship. It lacked a liturgical calendar and specific places for worship. The religion developed as a reaction to a developing situation. There were no temples and no priests. Like his father Abraham, Isaac built an altar to God as a form of worship and invoked his name. Similar to most of the altars in the book of Genesis, the altar that Isaac built had no sacrifices. Prayers and swearing are a simple, spontaneous outpouring of the heart and are not connected to a site or a cult. They were individual and tailored for a specific purpose. Blessings are pronounced by God, but also by individuals. Isaac is the first patriarch that blessed his sons. The source of the power of a blessing is God. The custom of circumcision was an ancient one and was also practiced by the Egyptians. In Genesis, all of Abraham's descendants are circumcised. Isaac is the first person who is circumcised at eight days old. Later, the Hebrew Bible uses a negative tone while describing the uncircumcised. Reading the book of Genesis reveals that there is no religious antagonism. There is no mention of conflict with idolatry. Furthermore, there appears to be no major religious differences between the belief of the patriarch Isaac and his neighbors. Therefore, when Isaac and Abimelech completed the pact they were swearing to each other. Rebekah's family blessed her with the same blessing that Abraham received. Circumcision was practiced in the ancient world and only later did it become a mark of distinction between Israel and its neighbors. This difference of beliefs between the Israelites and their neighbors will become more apparent only after the covenant at Sinai. From that point on, Israelites inhabit one side of the world, with Gentiles on the other side. The religious customs

28. Attridge and Oden, *Philo of Byblos*, 57. no.1 33–34.

29. According to Sasson, the practice began among the NW Semites and then moved to the south where the Egyptians adapted it. According to him, circumcision was known to the inhabitants of North Syria during the early third millennium (Sasson, "Circumcision in the Ancient Near East," 473–76).

which appear in Genesis point to a distantly primitive stage of the Israelite religion, which was similar to Israel's neighbors.[30] In Genesis, we have the first steps toward monotheism that developed fully only after Israel received its laws and commandments.

Now that we have dealt with the religious customs of the patriarch Isaac, the next stage of our study is to consider whom Isaac worshipped. The different names for God and the form of God's appearance will be examined.

---

30. For a different view, see Van Seters, "Religion of the Patriarchs," 220–33.

5

Whom Did Isaac Worship?

THE FIRST TIME THE name Yahweh is mentioned in Genesis 2:4 is when the first man invoked the Lord (Yahweh) by name. In other words, monotheism was the first original religion of the human race. Later, according to Genesis 12:1, Yahweh called Abraham to leave his native land. Yahweh was also known to the other patriarchs who built altars to him and invoked his name. However, this tradition differs from the book of Exodus, which says the initial revelation of the name Yahweh took place during the time of Moses: "I am Yahweh; I appeared to Abraham, Isaac, and Jacob as El Shaddai, but by my name Yahweh I did not make myself known to them" (Exod 6:2–3). Although it was Yahweh who appeared to the patriarchs, they did not know him by that name. It is noteworthy that proper names mentioned in the Torah prior to the time of Moses are not constructed with the divine element based on this name. Thus, names with a prefix *yeho/yo* or suffix *yahu/yah* started to appear only after the birth of Moses. The Hebrew name of Moses' mother, יהוכבד *Yokheved*, is the first of these types of names. Hence, the current chapter examines the different names describing God's theophany. We will answer the question: Whom did Isaac worship? Did Isaac worship Yahweh or did he worship other gods? In addition, we will study the different forms of God's appearances, whether God appeared directly to Isaac or spoke to him through the medium of dreams. Furthermore, was it God or an angel who revealed himself to Isaac?

ISAAC

THE WORSHIP OF ELIM

According to Exodus, the patriarchs knew God mainly as El Shaddai. El Shaddai is the most common name constructed with the initial prefix "El." The epithet "Shaddai" appears alone or in combination with 'El.' The term "El Shaddai" appears mostly in poetic texts, which testify to its antiquity since Hebrew poetry tends to preserve the earliest forms of language.[1] Furthermore, there are only two names in the Hebrew Bible constructed with the element Shaddai: Zurishaddai and Ammishaddai.[2] Although the text in Exodus says that Yahweh appeared to the patriarchs as El Shaddai, examination of the Isaac cycle shows otherwise. The name "El Shaddai" is not mentioned with Isaac.

El Shaddai was not the only El that the patriarchs worshipped. All accounts agree that the patriarchs worshipped different Elim. El is common to all Semitic languages as a general term for god. The etymology of "El" is uncertain and perhaps derives from a Semitic root, "to be strong." The patriarchs worshipped God under the name El, thus "El Elyon" (Gen 14:18–22), "El Olam" (21:33), "El Roi" (16:13), "El-elohei Israel" (33:20), "El Bethel" (31:13; 35:7), and "El Shaddai" (17:1; 28:3; 35:11; 43:13; 48:3; 49:25). Examination of these titles shows they are connected to certain locales: El Beth El to Beth El, El Olam to Beer-sheba, El Roi to a sanctuary farther south near Kadesh, and El-elohei Israel to the vicinity of Shechem. On the other hand, El Elyon and El Shaddai do not correspond to a place.

Isaac is not mentioned as worshiping one of the "*elim*." Nevertheless, it is more than likely that he worshipped "El Roi" and "El Olam." El Roi is mentioned for the first time after the angel's revelation to Hagar. At this site God promised her a son, Ishmael. She called the Lord who spoke to her "El Roi" and named the place Beer-lahi-roi (Gen 16:14). Later, Isaac settled in this place, which might be a symbolic declaration of his supremacy over his brother Ishmael (25:11). Isaac is the one who was chosen to be blessed and Ishmael to be supplanted. Since Isaac lived there he probably worshipped El Roi, who was the local deity. The place is mentioned again in Genesis 24:62–63, where we read that Isaac came back from Beer-lahi-roi where he was walking in the fields. He probably went to Beer-lahi-roi to pray for

---

1. Sarna, *Exploring Exodus*, 51.

2. "Zurishaddai" means "My Rock is Shaddai," and "Ammishaddai" means "My Kinsman is Shaddai." Both names belong to two Israelites who were born in Egypt. Interestingly, the second name was discovered in a hieroglyphic inscription from fourteenth-century-BCE Egypt. See Cross, *Canaanite Myth and Hebrew Epic*, 53.

the success of the servant's mission to bring him a wife. Among modern scholars it is Noth who claims that Isaac and Ishmael both used the well water of Beer-lahi-roi and participated in the cult of the deity where El-Roi (Gen 16:3) was worshipped.[3] According to him, Isaac and Ishmael were "brothers" by the fact that the two clan groups used the same water resources of Beer-lahi-roi, worshipping the same deity there. It is because of this connection that the figure of Ishmael enters the patriarchal tradition.[4] However, based on the biblical text this cannot be proven. The information that is given in Genesis 24:62 and 25:11 shows that Isaac has an association with Beer-lahi-roi. It is possible that Isaac received theophany at this site, but this tradition was lost. The patriarchs were seminomads, so they took their patron deity from place to place as they moved. It was later that the patron deity of the patriarchs would become localized at the place that became more important to the tribe or to the patriarchs.[5]

Isaac probably also worshipped El Olam. This deity is already mentioned with Abraham. It was in Beer-sheba where Abraham invoked the name of the Lord as the Everlasting God, "El Olam," which is a divine epithet. To call on the name of a god means to worship that god. In the pre-Israelite period, El Olam was worshipped in Beer-sheba. Cross points to the Ugaritic parallel *mlk 'lm*.[6] The Ugaritic texts do not mention the title El-Olam, but they mention *špašu' lm*, "Sun the everlasting."[7] The title *'el du 'olam* "El the eternal one" was found in an inscription at Serbit el-Khādem from the fifteenth century BCE, and "the goddess, the everlasting," *'lt 'olam* appears as late as the seventh century BCE in the Phoenician incantation text from Arslan Tash.[8] It should be noted that this can also mean the "everlasting oath."[9] It appears that the epithet "the Everlasting God" existed in antiquity and was not unique to the Bible. As Jenni pointed out: "One may conclude from the brief notice in Gen 21:33 that there existed a pre-Israelite cult of *'el 'ōlām* which the Israelites transferred to Yahweh."[10] We

---

3. Noth, *History of Pentateuchal Traditions*, 108.
4. Ibid., 108–9.
5. Lutz, "Isaac Tradition," 237.
6. Cross, *Canaanite Myth and Hebrew Epic*, 13–30.
7. *KTU* 2.42.
8. *KAI* 27:9–10; Cross, "Yahweh and the God," 236–41.
9. See de Pury, "EL-OLAM," 290.
10. Jenni, "Das Wort 'ōlām," 197–248; Jenni, "Das Wort 'ōlām," 1–35; Jenni, "'ōlām," 858.

believe that it was probably practiced privately in family surroundings, in contrast to the later official Yahwistic national religion. Since Isaac lived in Beer-sheba he probably was familiar with the cult of El Olam and worshipped him.

The mention of the different *Elim* in Genesis points to an earlier phase of worshipping God. When the first Hebrews moved into Canaan, they found altars and sanctuaries where El was worshipped. Since El had many traits in common with their own clan deity, they identified him with their own God.[11] The Canaanite El was assimilated into the biblical concept of God at an early stage in the patriarchal narrative. Thus, when Abraham meets Melckizedek, the king of Salem, he uses one of El's lofty titles, El Elyon, the "God Most High," for his own God Yahweh (Gen 14:22). Hagar identifies El Roi, the "God of Seeing," with Yahweh (16:13). Abraham, after he planted a tree at Beer-sheba, uses the epithet El Olam, "the Everlasting God" for Yahweh. Jacob named his resting place in Beth El, the "House of El" (28:12–19). The fusion between El and Yahweh took place at an early stage; this is probably the reason why there is nothing negative about El, even though he was worshipped by the Canaanites. Conversely, Baal, the Canaanite god of storm and fertility, is condemned time after time in the Hebrew Bible. Baal is the chief rival of Yahweh, who led the Israelites astray from their covenant with God.

YAHWEH

In contrast to the previous section where we assumed that Isaac worshipped El Roi and El Olam, the Bible tells us clearly that Isaac was familiar with the name Yahweh. Accordingly, Isaac received theophany in the area near Gerar. In that theophany Yahweh told him to remain in the land and promised to be with him and bless him. Gerar is important because of the theophany; nevertheless, Gerar did not become a cultic center. It is possible that at first the place was important for Isaac and his clan, but it lost

---

11. Genesis shows that the characteristics of the biblical El are very similar to those of El in the Canaanite epics from Ugarit. In these, El is the king of gods. His description resembles the god El that the patriarchs worshipped. El is the creator of the universe, the creator of the human race, and the father of gods and humans. His attributes as kind and compassionate are the same as the biblical El. He lives on a mountain from which all the fresh water comes to the world. He also lives in a tent and not a temple. In the epics of Kirta and Aqhat, he is the one who provides offspring to the childless couple. See Pitard, "Before Israel," 73–74.

its importance with the emergence of Beer-sheba as the major important cultic center. Indeed, Yahweh is mentioned in the second theophany in Beer-sheba: "That night Yahweh appeared to him and said, I am the God of your father Abraham..." (Gen 26:24). The epithet "the God of your father" appears here for the first time. It conveys continuity between Abraham and Isaac. The God who spoke to Abraham affirms his promises to Isaac, who is the heir of the blessing. Upon receiving the divine message, Isaac invoked God by the name "Yahweh" and he built an altar there.

From the description of the theophany it appears that Beer-sheba was an important cultic place. The importance of Beer-sheba is also mentioned with Jacob who stopped at Beer-sheba and made sacrifices to the God of his father Isaac (Gen 46:1). It is noteworthy that only Isaac is invoked here, probably because he is the one who built the altar at Beer-sheba and received the theophany there. De Pury suggests that Beer-sheba was the most important place and it was the cultic center of the "Isaacite" tradition.[12] The tradition about the sacredness of Beer-sheba was also known in the north. Therefore, the prophet Amos mentioned it alongside Bethel and Gilgal (5:5–6; 8:14). The prophet denounced the "high places of Isaac" which most likely included Beer-sheba (7:9).

THE GOD OF MY/YOUR/HIS FATHER

The phrase "the God of my/your/his Father," with the names Abraham, Isaac, or both, is found only in the patriarchal stories, which point to the close relationship between the patriarch and God. This epithet, as mentioned before, was first used when God appeared to Isaac: "I am the God of your father Abraham" (26:24), and later to Jacob in his dream at Beth El: "I am the Lord, the God of your father Abraham and the God of Isaac" (28:13). This formula is also mentioned in God's revelation to Moses: "I am, he said, the God of your father, the God of Abraham, the God of Isaac, and the God of Jacob" (Exod 3:6). The use of this formula stresses the continuity between the patriarchs and Moses. There are some instances where the formula, "the God of my/your father," is mentioned without the name of the patriarch (Gen 31:5, 29; 43:23; 46:3; 49:26). Lewy was the first to point out that the phrase "God of the father" was well known in the ancient Near East over a long period from the nineteenth century BCE on.[13] The phrase "god

---

12. de Pury, *Promesse divine*, 189–91.
13. Lewy, "Les textes paléo-assyriens," 29–65.

of the father(s)" appears with and without accompanying a personal name. Thus, we find: "Ashur god of my father," "Ashur and Amurrum the gods of our father," and "Shamash the god of my father."[14] Evidently, the phrase "the God of my/your/his Father," attested to in the patriarchal narrative as well as in the ancient Near East, came to indicate the close relationship between the individual and his god, who was his patron and protector. It was typical for a nomadic society to look for an intimate god who would guide and protect them.

PATRON DEITY

The fact that the patriarchs had personal ties with God is manifested also in titles such as: "the God of Abraham"[15] (Gen 28:13; 31:42, 53), the "Fear of Isaac," (31:42; 53) and "Mighty One of Jacob" (49:24).[16] God was the patron deity of the clan. Therefore, when Laban and Jacob formed a pact, each side invoked his own deity. Laban swore by the God of Nahor, while Jacob swore by the Fear of Isaac. Alt suggested that the patriarchal gods did not bear their own name but were named for their cult founder. To bolster his claims, Alt pointed to the Nabatean and Palmyrean inscriptions from the first century BCE to the fourth century CE.[17] The inscriptions describe nomadic people who worshipped "the god of X," where X was the name of the founder of the cult. However, we should note that the patriarchal period is too remote from the Nabatean period to make a valid comparison. Alt further says that the cults of theses deities were restricted to certain locals and sanctuaries. He concluded that the cult of the "Mighty one of Jacob" was worshipped among the tribe of Joseph, "the Fear of Isaac" among the tribes of Judah and Simeon, and "the god of Abraham" in the clan of Caleb and in the tribe of Judah.[18] However, as noted by many scholars there is no basis for this theory.[19] More than likely, the titles that the patriarchs gave to

---

14. Sarna, *JPS Torah Commentary: Genesis*, 396.

15. It was suggested that the name was "the Shield of Abraham" on the basis of Genesis 15:1. See Hyatt, "Yahweh," 130.

16. "Mighty One of Jacob" appears elsewhere only four times and in poetic text (Isa 49:26; 60:16; Ps 13:2, 5). It is similar to the Akkadian divine title *bel abāri*, "endowed with strength."

17. Alt, "God of the Fathers," 30–45.

18. Ibid, 25–30.

19. Haran, "Religion of the Patriarchs," 51n34; Wenham, "Religion of the Patriarchs," 172–73.

their God were merged by the literary editors into the God of Israel. Their epithets disappeared and they are found under names such as the "the God of your fathers," and "the God of Abraham, Isaac, and Jacob."

There are two references to פחד יצחק *paḥad yitsḥak*, which is usually translated as "fear of Isaac" (Gen 31:42, 53). The first is mentioned by Jacob when he complains about Laban's mistreatment of him. Accordingly, if it had not been for his father's God, the God of Abraham and *paḥad yitsḥak*, Laban would have sent him away empty-handed. In the second occurrence, Jacob takes an oath by *paḥad yitsḥak* while Laban takes an oath by the God of Abraham and the god of Nahor. Hence, the question that arises is: What is the meaning of this expression "*paḥad yitsḥak*?" Also, what is its function in the narrative? The most common interpretation for *paḥad yitsḥak* is "the Fear of Isaac," based on the Hebrew word *paḥad*, which means "fear." Albright pointed out that *paḥid* or *paḫd* originally meant "thigh, hip loins" in Arabic, Hebrew, and Aramaic. In Palmyrene, the word *paḫâ* means "family, clan, and tribe," and in Arabic, *faḫid*, according to native lexicographers, means "a small branch of a tribe consisting of a man's nearest kin."[20] Hence, he suggested rendering "the kinsman of Isaac."[21] Dahood went further and explained the word *paḥad*, which is found in Isaiah 24:18, Jeremiah 48:43, Psalm 91:5, Job 15:21, 22:10, and 39:22, Proverbs 3:25, and Song of Solomon 3:8 means "clan, flock, kinsman."[22] However, this interpretation is not convincing because the phonetic shift of the Arabic ذ is the Hebrew ז zain and not ד dalet.[23]

A more recent proposal was suggested by Koch and followed by Malul.[24] According to Malul, the word *paḥad* is Aramaic for "thigh." The thigh is a euphemism for the genitals, symbolizing the family and the ancestral spirit of Isaac. In the patriarchal stories, twice there is mention of an oath by the thigh. The oath was taken at a time of crisis. The spirits of the family were summoned by a symbolic gesture accompanying the oath and called on to protect their descendants. However, this explanation which suggests Jacob swears by his "father's thigh" must be rejected since the formula "put the hand under the thigh" (Gen 24:9) is missing from our verse.

---

20. Albright, *From the Stone Age*, 248n71.
21. Ibid., 248.
22. Dahood, *Ugaritic-Hebrew Philology*, 69n2035.
23. Hillers, "Paḥad Yiṣḥāq," 90–92; Levine, "*paḥad yiṣḥāq*," 451–52.
24. Koch, "Pǎḥād Jiṣḥaq,"107–15; Malul, "More on the Paḥad Yiṣḥāq," 192–200.

ISAAC

There is no need to change the meaning of *paḥad* as "fear," as it refers to the dread accompanied by God's appearance. The "fear of Isaac" is one of the attributes of the God of Isaac. His powers sent terror among all his enemies. Indeed, in the Bible we read about terror from the Lord (1 Sam 11:7; Isa 2:10). Additionally, fear arises from God's theophany and is carried over into the cultic context of worship: "Serve Yahweh with fear, and rejoice with trembling" (Ps 2:11)! It is more than likely that *paḥad yitsḥak* refers to the God that Isaac turns to in times of threat as we find in Hosea 3:5: "and they will thrill over the Lord and over his bounty in the days to come." Therefore, Jacob's sayings in Genesis 31:42 mention *paḥad yitsḥak* as a reference to the God who protects him.[25] Indeed, Jacob's family god is mentioned in verses 24 and 29, as threatening Laban to not harm Jacob. *Paḥad yitsḥak* was a deity that was known within the circles of Isaac by the name of the patriarch who received the revelation and established the cult. As with the other divine names in the book of Genesis, this title was later conceived as a title for Yahweh. In other words, before Moses, Yahweh revealed himself with different names to the patriarchs.

WORSHIPING ONE GOD

According to Frank Moore Cross, the different divine names in the book of Genesis do not point to different gods worshipped by the Hebrews before they adopted Yahwism.[26] He believes they are different titles of "El" through the pre-Mosaic period. He suggests continuity between the patriarchal religion, a form of "El" religion, and the Yahwism, which was accepted later by the Israelites. However, we believe, as mentioned before, that the Canaanite "El" was assimilated into the biblical concept of God at an early stage in the patriarchal narrative. When the patriarchs and the first Israelites came to Canaan they made "the language of Canaan" their own (Isa 19:8). Thus, not surprisingly, the terms that they used to describe their God were similar to that of the Canaanites. The patriarchs contextualize their theology to match their situation, so they select a name for God that matches their particular need at that moment in time. Each name and phrase had a different meaning and referred to God's different attributes. For the sages, the ancestors of Israel were true monotheists. Most telling is a midrash that grapples with

---

25. Levine, "paḥad yiṣḥāq," 452.
26. Cross, "Yahweh and the God," 225–59.

the different names of God. According to this midrash, the different names of God point to different attributes of God:

> R. Abba. b. Mammel said: God said to Moses: "Thou wishest to know My name. Well, I am called according to My work; sometimes I am called 'Almighty God,' 'Lord of Hosts,' 'God,' 'Lord.' When I am judging created beings, I am called 'God,' and when I am waging war against the wicked; I am called 'the Lord of Hosts.' When I suspend judgment for man's sins, I am called 'Adonai' for 'Adonai' refers to the attribute of Mercy, as it is said: The Lord, the Lord (Adonai, Adonai), God, merciful and gracious."[27]

THEOPHANY

In the biblical stories, the purpose of revelation is to make man know God. Revelations show humanity God's power, nature, glory, plans, and his will. The vocabulary that describes God's revelations uses words such as "to see," "hear," "perceive," "to understand," and "to know." In each revelation, God tells man about himself—who he is, about his acts in the past, what he will do, and what he requires them to do. Therefore, God revealed his plans and expectations to Noah and Abraham (Gen 6:13–21; 12:1; 15:13–21; 17:15–21; 18:17). Each revelation was needed because God is transcendent. He is far from man and man can neither see him nor find him.

God spoke and appeared to the three patriarchs. At first, outside of the land of Israel, Abraham only heard God's voice. God only appeared to him upon arrival in Canaan (Gen 12:7). To describe God's theophany, the Hebrew Bible uses the verb ראה *rā'â*, "to see." This verb appears several times in the Abrahamic cycle (12:7; 17:1; 18:1). In Genesis 12 and 17, God appears to Abraham, while in chapter 18, God is joined by angels. Similarly, the Bible used the verb "to see" when God revealed himself to Isaac: "The Lord had appeared to him and said . . ." (26:2); "That night the Lord appeared to him and said . . ." (v. 24). On two occasions God appeared to Isaac and spoke to him. Jacob, on the other hand, received his revelations in the form of dreams (28:12–18; 31:10–13; 46:1–4). Only in one incident are we told that God appeared to him (35:9). In addition, he had encounters with angels, first in his dream at Beth El, then on his way back to Canaan (32:20), and finally in Jabbok where he wrestled with an angel of God (32:25–30).

---

27. *Exod Rab.* 3:6.

Isaac

Despite the fact that the Bible describes God's theophany with "to see," "Yahweh let himself be seen," and "showed himself," in most cases, there is no attempt to describe his form or appearance—only the words that were spoken are mentioned. Evidently, the spoken words were more important than the theophany was.[28] It is also possible that describing God's appearance was too difficult, thus his appearance is limited to only a few passages. Harold Rowley suggests that "in the teaching of the Old Testament, God is nowhere conceived of as essentially in human form. Rather is he conceived of as pure spirit, able to assume a form rather than as having in himself physical form."[29] However, there is no evidence to support this assertion. The description of God's appearance to the patriarchs is a form of speech and it does not mean that they saw him face to face; it conveys the idea that they received a message from God.

As noted above in two passages, we read that God appeared to Isaac, thus, the question arises as to the nature of the theophany (Gen 26:2, 24). In the first incident the text tells us that God appeared to him (Gen 26:2). The description here is characteristic of the ancient Near East and to the biblical narrative where we read about the encounter between man and God. This divine revelation is introduced by the Hebrew וירא *va-year'*, "the Lord appeared." It is noteworthy that the formula "the Lord appeared" is distinctive to the Genesis patriarchal narrative and is used three times with Abraham (12:7; 17:1; 18:1), twice with Isaac (26:2, 24), and once with Jacob (35:9). In Isaac's theophany, God forbade him to go to Egypt. In addition, he reaffirms to Isaac the covenant he made with Abraham. The promise of the land and promise of many descendants is mentioned here, in addition to the mention of God's promise, "I will be with you" (v. 3). The fact that God appeared to Isaac does not mean that Isaac saw God face to face, but it conveys the idea that he received a message from God.[30] God is beyond

---

28. Barr, "Theophany and Anthropomorphism," 32.

29. Rowley, *Faith of Israel*, 75–76.

30. According to the Hebrew Bible, the only person who saw God face to face is Moses: "When a prophet of the Lord arises among you, I make myself known to him in a vision, I speak with him in a dream. Not so with my servant Moses; he is trusted throughout my household. With him I speak mouth to mouth, plainly and not in riddles, and he beholds the likeness of the Lord" (Num 12:6–8). Moses is a unique prophet since, according to this text, he speaks directly to God, "mouth to mouth" or "face to face." There is nothing between them when Moses hears God's voice. Moses sees God's form in clear view. Nevertheless, even though God is close to Moses, Moses does not see God's face. This is stated in Exodus 33:20: "But He said, 'you cannot see my face, for man may not see me and live.'" In other words, by nature, human beings, including Moses, cannot

description, yet human nature demands that we attempt to describe God. The Bible does not describe things in terms of objective truths known only to God, but in terms of human understanding. This in turn led men to resort to the language of anthropomorphism. God addresses mankind in a manner accessible to their understanding and their own experience; this is what the Talmud means when it says, "The Law speaks with the tongue of man"[31]:

> Thus, when the Creator wished to describe Himself, He described Himself as provided with eyes, because men are familiar with the sense of sight and know from their own experience that its seat is the member of the body which is the eye, not because He really is provided with bodily members. Likewise, when He wished to let them know that no sound is veiled from Him, He described Himself as provided with ears, because among men sounds are perceived by the sense of hearing. The same applies to all matters of this sort.[32]

The second theophany occurs at *night* (26:24). In addition, it introduces the formula "I am the God of your father Abraham." Mentioning the time of the theophany is typical to the dream phenomenon, thus we read: "But God came to Abimelech in a dream by night" (Gen 20:3) or "but God came to Laban the Aramean in a dream by night" (31:24). Later we read "that night God came to Balaam" (Num 22:20). Each time God appears at night to gentiles. Nevertheless, even when the dreamers are Hebrews, the Bible consistently reports that the dreams are nocturnal. During Jacob's dream in Bethel, "he came upon a certain place and stopped there for the night, for the sun had set" (Gen 28:11). Similarly, "at Gibeon the Lord appeared to Solomon in a dream by night" (1 Kgs 3:5). Unlike the Bible, however, the ancient Near East seems to have attached no great importance to a dream's timing. This detail is omitted from most dream narratives in that literature.

The self-introductory formula is another typical element of dream theophany. Therefore, when God appeared to Isaac, the text says: "I am the God of your father Abraham" (Gen 26:24). Similarly, God identifies himself in Jacob's dream at Bethel: "He said, I am the Lord, the God of your father Abraham and the God of Isaac" (28:13); "I am the God of Bethel" (31:13).

---

directly observe God. See Levine, *Numbers 1–20*, 341–42.

31. *b. B. Meṣ*, 31b.

32. Nemoy, *Karaite Anthology*, 63.

ISAAC

The inclusion of the Lord's name is meant to suggest that there is a close relationship between the deity and the dreamer. That is, the deity is the dreamer's patron and protector. In extrabiblical sources, as well, there are dreams in which the deity identifies himself. For example, in the dream of Thutmoses IV, we read, "I am your father, Harmakhis-Khepri-Re-Atum."[33] And in another Egyptian dream, that of Djoser, we read, "I am Khnum, your creator."[34]

The other element that is typical to a message dream is the message itself, which refers to the future. Here God tells Isaac: "Fear not, for I am with you, and I will bless you and increase your offspring for the sake of my servant Abraham" (26:24). The message starts with the formula "Fear not" which occurs numerous times in the Hebrew Bible and also in Jacob's dream (28:13 LXX; 46:3). It is also found in extrabiblical sources known as "oracles of assurance." It was given to a king before battle. For example, King Esarhaddon of Assyria (680–669 BCE) receives an oracle: "King of Assyria, fear not! The enemy of the king of Assyria I deliver to slaughter."[35] The second part of God's message to Isaac contained a blessing. Although the word "dream" is missing from the text, nevertheless the other components which are typical to the biblical message dream are here. Therefore, God's introductory formula, the mentioning of the time *night*, and the message are typical of the biblical dream phenomenon. There is no clear explanation as to why the Almighty should communicate with a sleeping person, rather than clearly and openly when the recipient is awake. Hence it is possible that nocturnal dream theophanies are meant to express the distance between human beings and God. God appears in dreams in order to moderate the shock or danger of direct waking revelation. The dream represents a more refined and sophisticated state in the development of religion than that reflected in a direct encounter with the deity.[36]

God's appearance to Isaac in a dream interrupts the stories about the rift between Isaac and Abimelech. The theophany in Beer-sheba, which is found in verses 23–25a, is a complete unit. It has a beginning ("He went up to Beer-sheba.") and it has an end after the theophany—Isaac built an altar invoking the name of Yahweh and pitched his tent there. There are some parallels to the Abrahamic tradition in Genesis 21:33; in that story

---

33. Oppenheim, *Interpretation of Dreams*, 251, sec. 8, no. 15.
34. Ibid., 251, sec. 8, no. 19.
35. Pfeiffer, "Oracles Concerning Esarhaddon," 450.
36. Bar, *Letter that has Not Been Read*, 2–3.

Abraham planted a tamarisk at Beer-sheba and called upon the name of Yahweh the Everlasting God. What stands behind these two stories is to stress the sanctity of Beer-sheba and its place in the cultic tradition of the Israelites.

ANGELOLOGY

Stories about angels' appearances to humans are typical to the patriarchal narrative and to the judges' period.[37] In the Isaac and Ishmael stories angels are mentioned several times. When the Bible needs to describe direct encounters with humans in a dramatic fashion, it uses angels. After the period of the judges, the appearance of angels diminishes. The last person who received a revelation from an angel was the prophet Elijah. With the development of classical prophecy, the prophet came instead of the angel. Only later, in prophetic vision, not only do we again encounter angels, but a new type of angel. The angels are no longer appearing to humans but are seen in visions. The Hebrew word for an angel is מלאך *malàkh*, derived from the stem *l-'k*, "to send." In Genesis, it is also used for ordinary humans (32:4). Later, a prophet or a priest might also be called "an angel of the Lord" (Hag 1:13; Mal 2:7).

There is not much we know about them; they are nameless, with no individuality or free will, and no hierarchy among them. Their main function is to deliver God's words, to be emissaries. In Israel, as in the ancient Near East, the angels were part of the royal court; Yahweh was envisioned as a king and the angels served in his royal court (Gen 28:12; 33:1–2). There are incidents where angels are perceived in human form; therefore, the people to whom they appear are not aware of their angelic nature. Abraham's three visitors are described as "men" (18:1, 16, 22:19:5, 10, 12, 16). Later, they are described as angels (19:1, 15); but the people of Sodom perceived them to be human (19:5, 9). A similar incident is described in the Samson story where an angel of the Lord appeared to Samson's mother. She describes him as a man of God who "looked like an angel of God, very frightening" (Judg 13:6). Her husband, Manoah, does not recognize him as an angel at first, and does so only after he disappears in flames on the altar (vv. 20).

When Hagar ran away from Sarah, the angel of the Lord appeared to her. As mentioned before, this is the first appearance of an angel in the Hebrew Bible. The angel of the Lord is mentioned four times in chapter 16

---

37. Indeed, one of the characteristics of the Jacob cycle is the encounter with angels.

(vv. 7, 9, 10, 11). The angel told Hagar that she would have a son and his name would be Ishmael. The angel speaks to Hagar (Gen 16:7–9, 11), but she responds to God (v. 13). There are some texts where the distinction between God and the angels is not clear. In some narratives, the angel appears to be a distinct figure, but later in the narrative, it appears as though it is Yahweh and not the angel.

Hagar had a second encounter with an angel, this time after Abraham expelled her and her son Ishmael. Like chapter 16, she was in the desert and the water was gone so she left her son under one of the bushes because she did not want to watch him die. She sat afar and burst into tears. It is God who heard the cry of the boy, but it was an angel of God that called Hagar from heaven. The angel told her that God heard the boy's cry and would make him a great nation. Then we read that God opened the eyes of Hagar and she saw the well of water.

The angel of the Lord is also mentioned in the binding of Isaac. At first God commanded the sacrifice of Isaac, but later Abraham is addressed by the angel of the Lord from heaven (22:1, 11–18). Angels usually travelled between heaven and earth (28:12), but the urgency of the moment required the angel to call from heaven. This is similar to the call of the angel to Hagar from heaven (21:17). The unclear demarcation between God and the angel is also found in the Moses story. The angel of the Lord appears to Moses in the burning bush (Exod 3:2), but Moses speaks directly with God in the rest of the story. In the Exodus story, it is God who leads the Israelites (Exod 13:21), then it is his angel (14:9). So, too, in the Gideon story, sometimes Gideon speaks with God and sometimes with the angel (Judg 6:11). From this, scholars infer that the angel was not an independent being but a manifestation of divine power and will. Since the angel is partly identified with God, he is his messenger; therefore, he uses God's name while speaking. Another possibility is that the phrase "angel of God" is an addition. At first, only the name "God" appeared in the stories. But the fear that the stories would be perceived as too corporeal necessitated the addition of the phrase "angel of the Lord." However, since this was not done consistently, there are difficulties. Indeed, this view was held by the *Maghāriyya*, a Jewish sect that flourished in Egypt and among the Karaites. Accordingly, all the anthropomorphic passages in the Bible are referring to angels, rather than to God. Furthermore, it was an angel who created the world and addressed the prophets.

In conclusion, at first glance it appears as though Isaac worshipped many gods. Isaac is connected with places such as Beer-lehi-roi and

Beer-sheba where El Roi and El Olam were the local deities. Since he lived in those locales, more than likely he was familiar with those *elim* and worshipped them. Isaac is also mentioned as worshipping "the God of the Father." The God of the Father is mentioned with the names Abraham, Isaac, or both. This epithet is used when God appeared to Isaac: "I am the God of your father Abraham" (26:24), and to Jacob in his dream at Beth El: "I am the Lord, the God of your father Abraham and the God of Isaac" (28:13). This formula is also mentioned in God's revelation to Moses: "'I am,' He said, 'the God of your father, the God of Abraham, the God of Isaac, and the God of Jacob'" (Exod 3:6). These phrases indicate the close relationship between the patriarchs and God. The personal ties between God and Isaac are also manifested in a title such as the "fear of Isaac" (31:42; 53), which refers to the dread that accompanies God's appearance. The "fear of Isaac" is one of the attributes of the God of Isaac. His powers sent terror among all of his enemies. When the first Hebrews moved into Canaan, they found altars and sanctuaries where El was worshipped. Since El had many traits in common with their own clan deity, they identified him with their own God Yahweh. So they selected a name for God that matched their particular need at that moment in time. Each name and phrase had a different meaning and referred to God's different attributes. God addresses mankind in a manner accessible to their understanding and their own experience. Thus, when the Bible says that God appeared to Isaac, this is a form of speech; in other words, he received a message from God. In two separate incidents Yahweh appeared to Isaac (26:2, 24). We believe that in the second theophany God appeared to Isaac in a dream (26:24). This form of communication came to moderate the shock or danger of direct waking revelation. Stories about angels' appearances to humans are typical to the patriarchal narrative and to the judges' period. Hence, we read of angels appearing in the stories of Ishmael and Isaac. However, the unclear distinction between God and the angel led scholars to infer that the angel was not an independent being but a manifestation of divine power and will.

Chapter 26 describes several incidents in the life of the patriarch Isaac where he appears as the main character. The chapter describes his migration to Gerar where he finds prosperity digging wells, as well as his expulsion from Gerar and the signing of a covenant with Abimelech. The stories have resemblances to the early stories about Abraham, hence we will examine these stories and see what stands behind them.

6

Isaac at Gerar

THE MAIN ISAAC TRADITION is found in chapter 26. Isaac plays a major role in the story here and it is centered on him, whereas in other stories Isaac appears as a secondary character. This chapter describes Isaac's agricultural ventures, his successes in digging wells, and his feuds with Abimelech, the king of Gerar. In other words, it paints a picture of Isaac's life in general. Scholars note that the stories about Isaac and Abraham share many similar elements.[1] Isaac, as did his father Abraham, went to Gerar during a time of famine. He dug wells and gave them the same names his father had given them, and he had feuds with Abimelech that ended with a signed pact. He also passed his wife off of as his sister. We will compare and contrast these stories and explore the reasons for this repetition.

It was suggested that chapter 26 is a collection of independent traditions and not a coherent unit. Noth maintains that chapter 26 does not convey the impression of something original, that it was developed gradually. This chapter includes several units of traditions which are outlined and not complete. The units were combined around the theme of "Isaac and the people of Gerar."[2] J collected all the material that was known to him from the oral tradition that pertained to Isaac. He believed that Isaac was prior to Abraham and was more important. Only late in the history of tradition did

---

1. Van Seters, *Prologue to History*, 268; Carr, *Reading the Fractures of Genesis*, 198–99.
2. Noth, *History of Pentateuchal Traditions*, 104.

Abraham take over with the narrative elements attributed to him.[3] This happened when he became the predominant figure in the south. The stories of the feuds with Abimelech, the digging of wells, and the wife-sister motif were first told about Isaac and only later were attributed to Abraham. Von Rad claims that most of the chapter is the work of J. There is no mention of Jacob and Esau and their rivalry, which led him to believe that Isaac's tradition was written in its ancient version without being harmonized with the large composition of the patriarchal stories.[4] He further said that Genesis 26:1–33 is "not a narrative but a mosaic of Isaac's stories."[5] Alternatively, there are scholars who point out the coherence of the material. Van Seters argues that the narrator of the Isaac story and the author of the promises are one and the same.[6] An examination of chapter 26 shows that in each episode, knowledge of the previous episode is presumed. Verses 1–11 and 12–33 include the same motifs and display structural counterparts that create a unified work.[7] Similarly, Blum and Nichol point to the coherence of all the material in verses 1–33. According to Blum, it is an "extraordinarily tightly composed narrative."[8] Nichol noted, "Each unit demands a certain amount of tacit knowledge which must be derived from previous unit."[9] Furthermore, according to him, there is no evidence that stories in chapter 26 existed independently as oral stories. Thus, we will examine the different episodes of chapter 26 and determine whether the chapter is a collection of originally independent traditions or if there is coherence to the chapter. In order to answer these questions, we will examine the structure and settings of chapter 26 and its place within the book of Genesis.

DESCENT TO GERAR

Because of the famine, Isaac went to Gerar (Gen 26:1). Famine had already been mentioned in the Abrahamic cycle where the patriarch went to Egypt to keep his family from starving (Gen 12:10). Later Jacob and his sons followed a similar path and went to Egypt because of the famine (Gen 41–47).

3. Noth, *History of Pentateuchal Traditions*, 103–4.
4. Von Rad, *Genesis*, 270.
5. Ibid., 269.
6. Van Seters, *Prologue to History*, 269.
7. Wenham, *Genesis 16–50*, 185.
8. Blum, *Die Komposition*, 302.
9. Nicol, "Studies in the Interpretation," 63.

Isaac

The function of the famine in these stories is to set in motion human events of interest. By contrast, in texts such as Deuteronomy 11:13–17, the famine is divine retribution. Indeed, in the Targum for Ruth, there is a list of ten famines that had occurred since creation. All of these famines were meant to punish people, although the Bible does not say so.[10] Famine was common all over the ancient Near East, which lends reliability to the story. Since Gerar is close to Isaac's place of habitat, Van Seters pointed out that going to Gerar "would be of no help at all." According to him, Gerar in Genesis 26:1 is taken from Gerar in 20:2 where famine is not mentioned.[11] Thompson, on the other hand, does not accept Van Seters's reasoning and says the famine in these stories has only a literary function.[12]

According to Rashbam (Rabbi Samuel ben Meir, ca.1080–1174), Isaac's original plan was to follow his father Abraham by going to Egypt to avoid the famine. The shortest road to Egypt was through Philistia (Exod 13:17). However, when he was on his way to Egypt, God appeared to him and ordered him not to leave the promised land. Similarly, Ramban suggests that Isaac intended to go to Egypt. However, before doing so, he went to his father's ally to see whether he could stay in his territory to avoid the need to go to Egypt. Ramban sees a great significance in the fact that Isaac stayed in Gerar. He believes that every event in the lives of the patriarchs is foreshadowing events in the future of their children. Thus, Abraham's stay in Gerar foreshadowed Isaac's stay in Gerar.

Abimelech is the king of Gerar and he is the king of the Philistines (26:1). Abimelech was already mentioned in chapter 20 as the king of Gerar; thus, the inevitable question becomes: Is this the same Abimelech that appears in chapter 26? The name Abimelech means "My father is king." The name Abimelech is mentioned later during David's time (Ps 34:1).[13] Again, the same name Abi-milki is mentioned as the name of the king of Tyre in the fourteenth century BCE.[14] Therefore, we believe that Abimelech is a dynastic name such as Pharaoh for the Egyptians. Examination of the biblical narrative shows that it is not the same person. The Abimelech of

---

10. *Ruth R.* 1.4.

11. Van Seters, *Abraham in History and Tradition*, 177.

12. Thompson, *Origin Tradition of Ancient Israel*, 55.

13. On the other hand, the name is found in the period of the Judges. Abimelech was the name of a son of Gideon by a concubine in Shechem (Judg 8:30).

14. Knudtzon, *El-Amarna-Tafeln*, 1556 (index to personal names); see 146:2 and 152:2.

chapter 20 enters the scene before Abraham is one hundred years old, while the Abimelech of chapter 26 comes after Abraham's death at age 175, when Isaac was sixty. There is at least seventy-five years' difference between the Abimelechs of chapter 20 and chapter 26. Evidently, we are dealing with two different personalities with the same dynastic name.

Abimelech is the king of the Philistines. It has been suggested that the mention of the Philistines in our story is anachronistic. According to extrabiblical sources, the Philistines arrived in the land of Canaan in 1200 BCE. The earliest reference to the Philistines comes at the time of Ramses II in the beginning of the twelfth century BCE. Starting with the book of Judges and later in the book of Samuel, the Philistines were the archenemies of the Israelites. These people, who are referred to in Egyptian sources as the "sea people," terrorized the Israelites for hundreds of years.[15] This led the Israelites to ask the prophet Samuel for a king who would fight their wars against the Philistines. The Philistines discovered the usage of iron, which gave them a major advantage on the battlefield. Saul, the first king of Israel, fought against the Philistines' domination throughout his life. In his last battle against the Philistines on Mount Gilboa, he died with his sons. Later it was King David who defeated the Philistines; after their defeat they served in his army.

The mention of the Philistines in Genesis is not anachronistic and is not a retrojection of a later period, but is authentic and reflects a historical reality. There were probably two waves of migration. The first wave arrived in Canaan during the patriarchal period. The second wave arrived in 1200 BCE after the Philistines were repelled by the Egyptians. More importantly, there are differences between the Philistines' portrayal in Genesis and later descriptions in the Bible. The Philistines in Genesis are not organized into five city-states led by Seranim. In Genesis, they live around Beer-sheba in the city of Gerar, ruled by a king. The local character and political structure all point to Abimelech as the ruler of a small enclave of the "Sea People" established in the Gerar area. Furthermore, the descriptions of the Philistines in Genesis reflect an early era when the relationship between the patriarchs and the Philistines was a peaceful one in contrast to the books of Judges and Samuel.

The patriarchs Abraham, Isaac, and Jacob traveled to the same sites. They journeyed to areas that were suitable for their seminomadic pastoral economy and convenient to small-scale trade. They moved their families

---

15. Singer, "Sea Peoples," 1059–61.

and possessions as the seasons dictated. In their travels, they were searching for water and pastureland. Their trips took place between great urban centers they lived near. From a geographical point of view, they lived near cites and in areas that were sparsely populated. These areas included central hill country and the Negev (viz., Shechem), Beth-El, Hebron, Beer-sheba, Gerar, and, in the Jacob stories, central Gilead. Beer-sheba, for example, is a constant stop during their travels. This is because Beer-sheba, in their time, was not a city, but was only a well. The patriarchs depended on those wells for their existence. During their migration, they passed by wells that belonged to their fathers. Clearly, this is the case with Isaac: "Isaac dug anew the wells which had been dug in the days of his father, Abraham and which the Philistines had stopped up after Abraham's death; and he gave them the same names that his father had given them" (Gen 26:18). What emerges from these descriptions is that Abraham, Isaac, and Jacob were seminomadic people who were often on the move. In times of famine, they dwelt among the Philistines and the Egyptians.

Nomadic societies included groups bound together by kinship. Not so with the patriarchs, who represent a single household that also included house-born slaves and herdsmen. The Abraham stories mention slaves, as do the Isaac stories. It has been suggested that a slave-based economy has no part in the nomadic way of life since there is no need for cheap labor.[16] Slave ownership existed in settled urban economic systems. Slaves were found in big households and in royal and temple estates. An examination of the Isaac stories reveals that he was practicing agriculture, and thus he needed slaves. Still, Isaac's endeavor into agriculture should not be viewed as a transition to agriculture. Nomads at Mari are described as engaging in small-measure agriculture from time to time. We believe that due to the famine, Isaac was forced to engage in agriculture. Furthermore, the favorable agricultural conditions directed him toward this new venture.[17]

In spite of engaging in agriculture, Isaac was on the move and he is the personification of the seminomadic people. We read that he pitched his tent (v. 25), which shows that he is also nomadic. Isaac had a powerful household, which included flocks and herds of cattle (v. 14). In addition, he had servants and herdsmen (vv. 19–20, 25, 32). In other words, Isaac was a prosperous farmer (v. 12) and affluent herdsman (v. 14).

16. Van Seters, *Abraham in History and Tradition*, 18.
17. Sarna, *JPS Torah Commentary: Genesis*, 185.

While staying in Gerar, Yahweh appeared to Isaac and ordered him not to go down to Egypt. Isaac is the only patriarch who did not leave the promised land. Based on this, the rabbis formulated the concept of necessity of living in the promised land. Isaac is the opposite of his father Abraham, who in a similar situation left for Egypt. God told Isaac "Reside in this land," (Gen 26:3) גור בארץ הזאת *gûr bā 'āreṣ hazzō 't* which is wordplay on the name of the place *Gerar*. Furthermore, גור *gûr* is also wordplay on גֵּר *ger*, which is a resident alien, a person with no legal rights who is dependent on the good will of the local people. It is noteworthy that the Hebrew word *gûr*, "to sojourn," means "to reside temporarily." The word "to sojourn" appears in the ancestral stories in Genesis, where each of the patriarchs leaves the land because of the famine but is not planning to settle in a foreign country permanently. Therefore, Abraham and Sarah sojourn in Egypt during a famine (12:10). When Joseph's brothers appeared before Pharaoh they told him: "We have come to sojourn in this land" (Gen 47:4). This statement is the basis for the saying in the Passover Haggadah that Jacob intended to stay in Egypt temporarily.

Because of Isaac's status as a resident alien, God encouraged Isaac and promised him, "I will be with you and bless you" (v. 3). But more likely, what we have here is the confirmation of the blessing that God gave to Abraham. The blessing God gave to Abraham is also given to Isaac. This includes the promise of the land and many descendants. These promises were the original content of the patriarchal tradition. The promises are expanded in verse 4. Isaac's descendants would be as numerous as the stars of heaven and receive all the lands. This blessing is followed by the promise of the blessing of the nations. This theme is also repeated to each of the patriarchs (Gen 12:3; 18:18; 22:18; 28:14). In other words, the blessing of the nations is connected with the destiny of Israel. The blessing is by virtue of Abraham's merit, so now it has passed to Isaac. In the past, when theophany occurred, an altar was built. This is not the case here; the text only mentioned that the revelation occurred in the vicinity of Gerar. Indeed, Gerar does not appear as a cultic center that was revered among the Israelites.

While staying in Gerar, Isaac sowed the land. He engaged in agriculture, a venture that requires a residence for a significant time. According to the midrash, the soil was hard and there was a drought.[18] Despite those difficult conditions, Isaac's crop was successful. He earned a bountiful harvest; his crop was one hundred times as much as was expected. He probably

---

18. *Gen. Rab.* 64:6.

sowed wheat which was cultivated in the land. It was planted during October and November, then harvested in May and June. Von Rad maintained that the harvest of a hundredfold is not an exaggeration.[19] On the other hand, Gunkel says that we have overstatement here; the wheat in the plains of Sharon yields about eight times, occasionally fifteen times.[20] Van Seters raised the question: How was Isaac, a sojourner, allowed to practice agriculture in the region of Gerar?[21] We have to remember that this land belonged to the inhabitants of Gerar. Furthermore, the text describes the hostility between the Philistines and Isaac. His theory is that Isaac enjoyed the privilege that was granted to his father Abraham by Abimelech to live in his land (Gen 20:15). Or, the author wanted the reader to think that Isaac had those privileges without saying it clearly. He did not want to portray Isaac as dependent on the king, which is what made him prosper; instead his prosperity is the result of God's blessings.[22]

Verse 13 describes the gradual growth of Isaac, which is the result of Yahweh's blessings promised to Isaac in verse 3. His wealth is in grain (v. 12) as well as flocks and herds (v. 14). Isaac's success in agriculture are in direct contrast to the beginning of the chapter where famine is mentioned. This success is the result of God's blessing. Isaac's abundant wealth in crops is unique to him. The emphasis on agriculture is rarely mentioned in Genesis (Gen 27:28; 30:14; 37:7). The other patriarchs, Abraham (12:16; 13:2; 24:35) and Jacob (30:43; 32:5, 15; 36:7), had their wealth characterized by multiplying livestock and servants.

Isaac's triumph in farming created tension with his neighbors. His wealth was visible to all and brought the envy of the Philistines. As a result, the Philistines stopped up all the wells that Abraham had dug and filled them with earth. Cutting the wells off threatened Isaac's herds. These wells were Isaac's inheritance from his father and were situated within the boundaries of Gerar. The narrator mentioned Abraham's name twice as the father of Isaac (vv. 15, 18) to stress that Isaac had a valid claim to these wells (21:25–30). Nevertheless, Isaac was expelled by Abimelech because of the wealth he acquired; the Philistines were envious of him, so he left (v. 17). Abimelech told Isaac, "Go away from us for you have become *too big for us* (עצמת)." The Hebrew word עצמת *āṣamtā* means "mighty strong," so

---

19. Von Rad, *Genesis*, 266.
20. Gunkel, *Genesis*, 295.
21. Van Seters, *Abraham in History and Tradition*, 188.
22. Ibid., 189.

the implication is that Isaac was very powerful in wealth and the size of his family. The king felt that Isaac posed a threat to his throne. These words by Abimelech foreshadow the story of the Israelites in Egypt, where the narrator, in stating that the Israelites posed a threat to the Egyptians, used the same Hebrew verb ויצצמו *wayyaʿaṣmû*: "they multiplied *and increased very greatly*" (Exod 1:7).

DIGGING WELLS

Chapter 26 describes Isaac's journey while digging wells in different places along the way. His journey starts at Gerar (v. 6) and includes him digging a well at wadi of Gerar (v. 17), in Esek (v. 20), in Sitnah (v. 21), and in Rehoboth (v. 22) before moving on to Beer-sheba (v. 23). Wenham pointed out that the word "encamped" appears only twice in the book of Genesis: once in our story (v. 17) and then in the Jacob story (33:18). Elsewhere it always refers to the Israelites camping in the wilderness (Exod 14:2; 19:2; Num 33:5–49). Therefore, he suggested that Isaac's life foreshadows the experience of his descendants.[23]

The Isaac stories contain a tradition about the patriarchs wandering in the western part of the Negev and their feuds with the Philistines about the wells. This description is typical of the "small cattle nomads." One group of nomads tries to expel and harm the other group by blocking up their wells. This portrayal suits the patriarchal period and its lifestyle. In that period, the existence of a group and its herd relied on watering holes. Thus, according to Westermann, the information about the wells was recorded. It included the location of the wells along with the route and the names of the wells; all of this was kept for the next migration.[24] This reality of living in the western part of the Negev is like what we read later about David and his people, who lived in that area under the protection of Achish the king of the Philistines.

As mentioned already, Isaac was expelled by Abimelech because he became too strong for the Philistines. This recalls Abraham's expulsion from Egypt (Gen 12:20). However, the motive for the expulsion is different. In Abraham's case he was rebuked and sent away with his wife and all that he possessed because of his deceit. On the other hand, Isaac was asked to leave because he was too powerful, although despite his power he did not

---

23. Wenham, *Genesis 16–50*, 191.
24. Westermann, *Genesis 12–36*, 426; See also Matthews, "Wells of Gerar," 123.

oppose Abimelech's order. Instead, he went and camped in the valley of Gerar. This place was probably not part of Abimelech's territory although it was situated in the Philistine land. Isaac stayed in the area that his father Abraham lived, redug the wells, and gave them the same names his father had given them. Isaac evidently knew the names of the wells and their locations. By giving the wells the same names, he asserts his right and ownership to the wells. As Rashbam pointed out, now no man could dispute his possession of them. He had to redig the wells because the Philistines had blocked them. While digging, the servants found a well of springwater; this new discovery led to a dispute between the herdsman of Gerar and Isaac's herdsmen. A feud over a well is already mentioned in the Abraham story, where the patriarch reproached Abimelech for the well his servants seized (21:25). Furthermore, in another episode we read of a feud between the herdsmen of Abraham and those of Lot. It appears that we have conflation of themes from the Abraham stories that were inserted into the life of Isaac.

Feuds over wells are not surprising since water has always been a very precious commodity in that part of the land, even today. Cornelius pointed out a similar text from Mari, which deals with disputes over water. Accordingly, one group appeals to the king to intercede on its behalf against another group so the water and ownership will be returned to them.[25] Isaac's herdsmen named the well they found *Esek*, which means "contention." In rabbinic terminology, the word means "in dispute with title ownership."[26] Isaac's herdsmen dug another well and there was a dispute over this well also. Isaac named the well *Sitnah*. The word *sitnah* is found only here and in Ezra 4:6; it refers to accusations contesting the right of another party. Radak related it to the word Satan: "adversary" or "hinderer." Accordingly, the word illustrates how the Philistines quarreled with him. The names that Isaac gave to the wells so far have a negative connotation. Still, in order to establish good relationships with his neighbors, Isaac moved again and abandoned the wells to the Philistines. He removed himself from the conflict. According to Radak he made certain that he would not be in the area where the Philistines would accuse him of digging in their territory. This generosity toward the Philistines recalls Abraham's kindness toward Lot (13:8–9). Isaac is portrayed as a peaceful person who did everything to keep peace between his camp and his neighbors.

25. Cornelius, "Genesis XXVI," 53–61.
26. *b. Ket* 93a; *b. Kam.* 9a; *b. Meṣ* 14a; *b. Šebu.* 31a.

Relocating to a new place changed Isaac's fortunes, so a third well was found. Since there was no quarrel, he named the new well *Rehoboth,* which has a favorable connotation. The meaning of this name is "a wide space for free movement." The place is identified with Ruheibeh, which is 30.5 km south of Beer-sheba. Several large wells which date to antiquity, as well as traces of agricultural efforts, are found in this area.[27] This part of the story about the three wells ends with Isaac praising the Lord.

ISAAC'S PACT WITH ABIMELECH

Isaac moved to Beer-sheba, the place where he lived with his father in the past, after he was almost sacrificed by him. He was expelled by Abimelech from Gerar. Nevertheless, Abimelech still felt uneasy with his presence being so close to his territory. Therefore, Abimelech came to meet Isaac in order to sign a pact with him. The king was accompanied by Ahuzzah, his councilor, and Phicol, the chief of his troops. The presence of the chief civilian and military officer shows the importance and significance he attached to the negotiation with Isaac. In the parallel account about Abraham and Abimelech, Ahuzzah is not mentioned at all; only Phicol appears in Genesis 21:22 and 21:32. To solve this discrepancy between the texts, the LXX inserts the words אחזת מרעהו *Ahuzzath mere'ehu* in Genesis 21:22 and 21:32; this was to create harmony between Genesis 26 and 21. On the other hand, the Jewish exegetes such as Onkelos translated *Ahuzzah mere'ehu* as "party of his friends." Thus, Abimelech appears here only with Phicol. This interpretation is also found in Genesis Rabbah and among medieval Jewish commentators.[28] Safren, on the other hand, pointed out the link between *mere'ehu* and the term *merḫûm,* which is mentioned in old Babylonian tablets from Mari.[29] Accordingly, *merḫûm* was supervisor of the royal pasture and he would report directly to the king on the welfare of the pasturage and the tribes using them. He would regulate the usage of the pasture. Since the biblical text deals with the conflict between the shepherds of Gerar and shepherds of Isaac over wells, this might explain the participation of Ahuzzath at the negotiations. Ahuzzath represents the branch of government that was responsible for the affairs of pasturage lands and shepherds' lands. As for Phicol, more than likely, it is not the same person that is mentioned

---

27. Sarna, *JPS Torah Commentary: Genesis,* 186.
28. *Gen. Rab.* 64:9.
29. Safren, "Ahuzzath and the Pact," 191.

Isaac

with Abraham since that event took place sixty years earlier. His title, "the commander of forces," appears in the Abraham and Isaac stories. Later the same title appears for commanders in Israel's early monarchial period (1 Sam 14:50; 26:5; 2 Sam 10:18).

The patriarch appears here as equal to the king. In contrast to previous episodes in Gerar, where Isaac was a guest, he now lives in his own territory and therefore felt freer to speak. Furthermore, the negotiations and the covenant ceremony were performed and initiated by Isaac. The patriarch raised the question: Why were they seeking his friendship even though they sent him away in an unfriendly manner? In response, Abimelech offered an apology and explanation. He realized that God has blessed Isaac; therefore, he was looking to have a covenant of peace with him.[30] He wanted to establish a good relationship with one who was blessed. Abimelech mentioned the incident in verses 7-11 where Isaac was allowed to withdraw in peace—no harm was done to him. For that reason, he expected that Isaac would not do any harm to them. He ended his proposal by referring to Isaac as "the blessed of the Lord." These words corresponded to the promise in verse 3: "I will be with you and bless you." The foreign king acknowledged that Isaac was blessed by Yahweh. Nevertheless, he ignored mentioning the feuds between his herdsmen and Isaac's herdsmen where his people stopped up the wells.

Despite past feuds and the hostile manner in which Isaac was treated in the past, a pact between the two parties was sealed, accompanied by a ceremonial meal. The pact came to regulate the relationship between Abimelech and Isaac. This recalled an earlier pact between Abimelech and Abraham (21:22-32). At that time the covenant was between these two individuals. This is not so in our episode where the narrator employs "we" and "us," since Abimelech is acting as a representative of his people. We find that Ahuzzath and Phicol took an active part in the covenant ceremony along with Abimelech: "Then he made for them a feast, and ate and drank" (Gen 26:30). The covenant between the two parties came to regulate the relations between two pastoralist groups and to allow Isaac to dig wells and pasture his flocks. The participation of both Ahuzzath and Phicol indicates the importance that Abimelech attached to this treaty. Ahuzzath appears here as the supervisor of pasturages, while Phicol the army commander could react with force against any violation of the treaty by Isaac. We believe

---

30. That Yahweh is with Isaac may be compared with that of Jethro (Exod 18:10-11); Rehab (Josh 2:9-11).

that the Philistines were concerned that Isaac's descendants would not see themselves as bound by the pact. The Philistines violated the covenant with Abraham and were worried that Isaac would break the covenant with them. Isaac's descendants could expel Abimelech's descendants from the land, so therefore, a covenant was needed to ensure future generations would not do this. Indeed, according to Westerman, this request for a pact by Abimelech makes sense only if Isaac represents the people of Israel.[31]

A meal was an integral part of covenant-making, where the person who offered the food admitted the other person into his own family.[32] In addition, it created a good atmosphere and harmony. Isaac, as the host, provided the meal, thus showing his good will. The meal was followed by a mutual oath the following morning. The oath probably also included a curse. This treaty put Isaac equal to the Philistinian king. Parenthetically, it is the king who initiates the pact, which might point to the fact that Isaac is not equal to the king but is the stronger party.

Earlier Abimelech sent Isaac away saying, "Go away from us" (v. 16). Later he claimed that he sent Isaac away in peace (v. 29). Here the roles are reversed; it is Isaac who sent Abimelech, but more importantly, he indeed sent him in peace. It is the first time in the patriarchal narrative that a dispute of this kind ends with a final peace.[33] This peace was possible due to God's blessings which he promised Isaac (v. 3) and was acknowledged by the king of the Philistines (v. 13). Accordingly, the peace here does not mean friendship, but means that the two parties can remain in a nonviolent relationship.

Remarkably, on the same day, Isaac's servants came to him informing him that they found a well. This is the fourth time that they found a well. This is not a coincidence; it is a further indication of God's blessings for Isaac. In contrast to previous times where Isaac's herdsmen had to abandon the wells, here they kept the well. Isaac named the well *Shiv'ah*, which is the feminine form of the number seven. Other ancient versions read differently (LXX read as "oath"; Syr., Vulg., Aquila, Symmachus "abundance"). Our story is very similar to an earlier episode that involves Abraham and Abimelech, where Abraham also named the well Beer-sheba (Gen. 21:22–34). In that story Abraham gave Abimelech seven ewes which, by accepting them, the king acknowledged Abraham's ownership of the well.

---

31. Westermann, *Genesis 12–36*, 429.
32. McCree, "Covenant Meal in the OT," 120–28.
33. Westermann, *Genesis 12–36*, 429.

ISAAC

Then Abraham and Abimelech took an oath and Abraham named the place Beer-sheba. In the Isaac story, on the same day that the patriarch and Abimelech took an oath, a well was discovered. Isaac named it *Shiv'ah*, and therefore, the name of the city is Beer-sheba. There is no reason for the number seven to be used in the Isaac story except if the author believed that seven animals were involved like in 21:28–29. Therefore, as mentioned previously, Isaac gave the wells "the same names that his father had given them" (v. 18). So, what we have here is wordplay on שבעה *Shiv'ah*, "seven," and שבועה *Shevu'ah*, "oath."

The stories about the well in Beer-sheba came to stress that the well belonged to the patriarchs and not to Gerar. The legends about Beer-sheba point to the holiness of the site. Abraham planted a tree there and there invoked the name of the Lord, the Everlasting God (Gen 21:33). Similarly, Isaac built an altar there and invoked the Lord by name (26:25). Both ancestors took an oath and God appeared to them. Following the footsteps of his father, Jacob, on his way to Egypt, stopped at Beer-sheba, offering sacrifices to the God of his father Isaac (46:1). Beer-sheba was a scared place long after the patriarchs and is mentioned in Amos's time (5:5; 8:14) where it was a pilgrimage and oath site (1Kgs 19:3).

SIMILAR STORIES

Scholars pointed to the parallels between the Abraham and Isaac stories. In these stories we read of the patriarchs that during the time of famine went and stayed in Gerar. The patriarchs passed their wives off as their sisters (see next chapter), dug wells, and had feuds with local inhabitants. Abimelech, the king of Gerar, was mentioned in the stories as expelling the patriarchs from his territory. Both Isaac and Abraham named the well Beer-sheba. The considerable overlapping between the stories led to the conclusion that there was narrative transferred from one story to another. Thus, our task is to determine what originally belonged to each story and the reason for this transfer. Based on these stories, Abraham and Isaac were related to each other. Isaac, however, is overshadowed by his father, Abraham, and later by his son, Jacob. According to Noth, an examination of the Abrahamic tradition shows signs of progression during the different stages of literary formulation from G ~ E to J.[34] Abraham is the "modern" figure and the duplicate stories belonged originally to Isaac rather than to Abraham. The stories were

---

34. Noth, *History of Pentateuchal Traditions*, 103.

first told about Isaac. Examination of the Abraham stories shows "narrative elements originally foreign to him."[35] The detailed information found in the Abrahamic stories was told first about Isaac.

However, examination of the Abraham and Isaac stories shows that the similarities between the stories are only on the surface. Analysis of the stories indicates that there are many differences between them, which emphasize the Abrahamic tradition as the original one. In the current story, Isaac went to Gerar because of the famine. In the story of Abraham in Gerar, no reason is given for Abraham's migration to Gerar; it is only in the first story about Abraham that we read that he went to Egypt because of the famine (Gen 12:10). Furthermore, in the Isaac tradition the narrator already has knowledge of the famine that took place in the time of Abraham and mentions it (Gen 26:1). In the Abrahamic cycle there is mention of only a single well that Abimelech's servants took from Abraham (Gen 21:25). In the Isaac stories, there is mention of multiple wells that belonged to Abraham which the Philistines filled with earth (26:15, 18). Isaac gave the wells the same names that his father had given them. Furthermore, we find that Isaac dug new wells. What we have here is the expansion of the tradition about the wells—not one well, but many. It was Gunkel who maintained that the stories about Isaac were the originals since they are short, and later they were expanded in the Abrahamic cycle. According to Gunkel, the briefer legend forms a complete unit, and more likely preserved the original forms.[36] However, as we can see, the stories about the wells shows otherwise. The Abrahamic cycle contains only brief information about the wells; it is the Isaac tradition which contains the more developed story.

At the center of the Isaac stories are themes of possession of arable land and disputes with the inhabitants over this arable land and its water resources. Isaac is the first patriarch who fulfills God's promise of the land since he is the first to cultivate it. Isaac, like his father, was originally a nomadic herdsman, possessing no land and seasonally changing the pasture he used. Here, in Gerar, he cultivated the land and received divine blessings for a plentiful harvest and prospering flocks and herds. Isaac, in contrast to Abraham, was engaging in an agricultural venture and had success doing so. He exemplified the natural process of nomads in the ancient world, which started the gradual evolution from nomad to farmers who sowed the land. Hence Abraham represented the past while Isaac represented the future.

---

35. Ibid., 104.
36. Gunkel, *Genesis*, xxviii–xxix.

Isaac

Isaac's expulsion from Gerar resembles Abraham's expulsion from Egypt (Gen 12:20). However, the causes for the expulsions are different in these stories. Abraham left Egypt after he was rebuked by Pharaoh for his deceit. Isaac, on the other hand, was asked to leave because he was too powerful.

The pact that Isaac signed with Abimelech has some similarities to the pact between Abraham and Abimelech, but there are also major differences. An examination of the stories reveals that there are expansions in the Isaac story; it is more developed than the Abrahamic story. The Abrahamic story is described with few details and its context is obscure. There is no link to the previous story of the expulsion of Hagar, so this story is independent. To solve this problem, Van Seters suggested that this episode be placed directly after Genesis 20:18.[37] In contrast, the Isaac story is connected to the theme of feuds over wells and there is a smooth transition between the feuds over the wells and the signing of a pact. Again, the pact between Abraham and Abimelech was between these two individuals. Not so in our episode where the narrator says that the pact was between Abimelech's party and Isaac. In the Abrahamic story the patriarch gave Abimelech sheep and oxen which are part of the pact-making ceremony. In addition, the narrator mentioned that Abimelech received seven ewes. In contrast, in the Isaac story we read of a ceremonial meal that Isaac prepared to seal the pact. In the Abrahamic story the place was named Beer-sheba because the patriarch and Abimelech swore an oath. Not so in the Isaac story, where the naming of the place has no connection to the pact between Isaac and Abimelech. Furthermore, the naming of the place comes after Abimelech and his party leave Isaac's camp.

There is no evidence of an oral tradition or a process by which the Isaac tradition was the first one, so as to serve as the origin for the Abrahamic tradition. An examination of the Isaac story shows it is a coherent one and there are links between the different parts. It starts with the story about Abimelech and Rebekah, later the feuds between Abimelech's shepherds and Isaac's shepherds, and in the end, the pact between Abimelech and Isaac. On the other hand, in the Abrahamic cycle, the story of Abimelech and Sarah is interrupted with the story of the birth of Isaac and the expulsion of Hagar and Ishmael. It is only after this episode we read of the pact between Abraham and Abimelech. We believe that at first they were independent stories about Abraham, who, while staying in Gerar, passed his wife off as his sister. Later there's a story about digging a well, his feuds with

---

37. Van Seters, *Abraham in History and Tradition*, 185.

the local inhabitants, and signing a pact with Abimelech. This was followed by naming a place Beer-sheba. These stories were told first about Abraham. It was only later that these episodes were told about Isaac. The narrator tied the stories together and created one homogenous story that is found in chapter 26. He achieved it by transferring parts of the Abraham story into the Isaac story by adding and changing some of the details in the stories.

STRUCTURE AND SETTING OF CHAPTER 26

At first glance, chapter 26 looks out of place in the biblical narrative. Chapter 25:20–34 recounts the story of the birth of Jacob and Esau. The story of the brothers and their rivalry resumes in chapter 27. There is no mention of the brothers in 26:1–33. Hence, without chapter 26, Genesis 25 and 27 would be more harmoniously joined. It was Fishbane who pointed out that chapter 26 balances chapter 34. Genesis chapter 34 interrupts Genesis 33 and 35. Chapter 34 describes the rape of Dinah and the actions that were taken by Jacob's sons. The chapter has no connection to Jacob's reconciliation with Esau and his return to Beth-el. Therefore, according to him: "The symmetry between Genesis 26 and 34 together with their parallel functions as interludes, thus preclude any assumption of haphazard editorial arrangement."[38] Furthermore, the chapters are linked by common themes of deception and strife. However, this explanation is unlikely. If chapter 26 serves as an interlude, and the brothers Jacob and Esau were already born, Rebekah could not have been passed off as a sister; the Philistines would recognize that she was a married woman. Therefore, the logical explanation is that the events which are described in chapter 26 took place before the birth of the twins.[39] Indeed, Nicol sees "Genesis 26:1–33 as a narrative that deals with the events in Isaac's life prior to the birth of his sons."[40] The story of the birth of Isaac's sons is an introduction to the cycle of the stories about Jacob and not a story about Isaac.

It was believed that our chapter is a collection of originally independent traditions; however, a close reading of the chapter shows otherwise.[41] As Van Seters points out, verses 1–11 and 12–33 include the same motifs

---

38. Fishbane, *Text and Texture*, 47.

39. Sarna, *JPS Torah Commentary: Genesis*, 184; Nicol, "Studies in the Interpretation," 15.

40. Nicol, "Chronology of Genesis," 337.

41. Noth, *History of Pentateuchal Traditions*, 104.

with similar structural components that produced a unified work. The individual episode has knowledge of the previous episode. The conflict that Isaac created with the Philistines by passing his wife off as his sister is paralleled by the conflict with the Philistines over the possession of the wells. Each time the conflict is resolved by Abimelech by edict (v. 11) and by treaty (vv. 28-29). This resolution is a testimony to God's promises to Isaac: "I will be with you and will bless you" (v. 3) and "I am with you; I will bless you" (v. 24).

Nicol points to the coherence of all the material in verses 1-33. According to him, "each unit demands a certain amount of tacit knowledge which must be derived from the previous unit(s)."[42] There is no evidence that the stories in chapter 26 existed independently as oral stories. The promises of the land, descendants, and the blessing to the nations, which are found in chapter 26, are found already with Abraham. The narrative structure includes three categories: "promise," "threat," and "resolution." The promise of progeny is threatened and resolved in verses 7-11; the promise of the land is threatened and resolved in verses 12-16, 17-23; the promise of the blessing for the nations is threatened and resolved in the Abimelech-Isaac treaty.[43] The motif of promises serves as the glue to the narrative story. The promise to the nations is the main interest of the author, who describes how Abimelech repented (vv. 16, 26-32).

As mentioned before, the events that involved Abimelech and Abraham are similar to the stories of Isaac and Abimelech. But more importantly, they are also themes from the early Abraham cycles, which are covered in chapter 26. The patriarch Abraham is mentioned eight times in chapter 26; by contrast, he is mentioned only fifteen times in chapters 27-50.[44] Wealth, which leads to quarrels between the patriarch's herdsmen and others, is mentioned in the Abraham and Lot story (13:2-10) as well as with Isaac and Abimelech (26:12-22). The separation between Lot and Abraham (13:11-12) is paralleled by Isaac and Abimelech (26:23). God's promise of many descendants is mentioned in 13:14-17 and also 26:24. Building an altar to God by Abraham (13:18) is similar to Isaac building an altar to God and invoking the Lord by name (26:25). Good relationships with foreigners are attested to in chapter 14; Abraham has three allies: Mamre, Eskhol, and Aner. He established a good relationship with Melchizedek as well. In

---

42. Nicol, "Studies in the Interpretation," 63.
43. Nicol, "Narrative Structure and Interpretation," 340.
44. Wenham, *Genesis 16-50*, 187.

Genesis 26:26–31, Isaac established a good relationship with Abimelech. Abraham was blessed by Melchizedek, a foreign king: "Blessed be Abram, God Most High, Creator of heaven and earth. And blessed be God Most High, Who has delivered your foes into your hands" (14:19–20). Similarly, Isaac was blessed by Abimelech, "From now on, be you blessed of the Lord!" (26:29).[45] All of these parallels between Abraham and Isaac come to show us the similarities and differences that exist between the Abraham and Isaac stories. By pointing to the resemblance between the Abraham and Isaac narratives, the author's aim is to stress the continuity between Abraham and Isaac. In other words, Isaac is the true heir to Abraham's legacy.

In conclusion, chapter 26 is our main source of information about the patriarch Isaac. This chapter contains several stories about the patriarch. It describes Isaac's agricultural venture, his success in digging wells, and his feuds with Abimelech, the king of Gerar. Isaac is the first patriarch that cultivated the land. Isaac typified the natural process of nomads in the ancient world evolving from nomads to being farmers. Abraham represents the past, Isaac the future. These stories about the patriarch Isaac are found already in the Abrahamic cycle. It was believed that narrative was transferred from one story to another. Despite the similarities between the stories there are also significant differences. An examination of these stories in the Abrahamic cycle shows that they are independent. Not so with the Isaac story, which is more developed and cohesive. The narrator borrowed the stories from the Abrahamic cycle and created one story by adding new dimensions to it. Genesis 26:1–33 deals with the events in Isaac's life prior to the birth of his sons. It describes different events that took place in the life of the patriarch. These events contain the same motifs and have similar structural components which produce a unified work. The individual episode has knowledge of the previous episode. This chapter exemplified the fulfillment of the promises that were given to Abraham. Isaac is the true heir to Abraham and he is an individual in his own right.

As previously mentioned, Isaac passed his wife Rebekah off as his sister. The story is very similar to two previous stories that took place in Egypt and Gerar, where Abraham passed his wife Sarah off as his sister. Therefore, in the next chapter we will examine these stories about Abraham and Isaac to see how similar or different they are.

---

45. Ibid.

7

Isaac's Wife-Sister

WHILE STAYING IN GERAR, Isaac deceives Abimelech, passing his wife Rebekah off as his sister (Gen 26:1–11). This is like his father Abraham, who twice passed his wife Sarah off as his sister (12:10–20; 20). In addition, the name of the king who was deceived is also Abimelech (chapter 20). These stories were believed to be three variations of a folktale; however, there is no consensus among scholars as to which of the three represents the oldest form of the story. Gunkel, for example, claimed that the account in 12:10–20 was the oldest.[1] Accordingly, some folkloristic features that are noticeable in this account are weaker in others. Genesis 20 is a "legend." It glorifies God and his help, there are no profane ideas, and there is no mention of Abraham's cleverness or Sarah's beauty. As for Genesis 26, he pointed out that there are neither "profane adventures" nor intervention by God, only implying that God protected Rebekah. In addition, he proposed that the story did not originate with the patriarch, but was a popular story transferred to the biblical narrative. According to him, the sequence of the stories is Genesis 12, Genesis 20, and then Genesis 26.

Noth, on the other hand, arrived at a different conclusion. He suggested the account in 26:1–11 is the oldest. He believed that the tradition about Beer-sheba and the south originated with Isaac, and only afterwards was transferred to Abraham.[2] This story about Isaac is distinct from the two

---

1. Gunkel, *Genesis*, 223–25; Skinner, *Genesis*, 365.
2. Noth, *History of Pentateuchal Traditions*, 102–9.

Abraham stories. It appears here in completely "profane" form.[3] There is no divine intervention which makes it closer to a folktale. Genesis 26 omits many details found in Genesis 12. The story is simpler and condensed, and specifics are left to the reader's imagination, so therefore he believed Genesis 26 was the oldest, containing the most original tradition, after which came Genesis 12:10–20, and lastly Genesis 20:2–18. Based on form criticism, it was suggested that the three episodes developed as oral alternatives of one original story.[4] In recent years scholars advocated that accounts B (Genesis 20) and C (Genesis 26) were literary arrangements based on A (Genesis 12).[5] In the current chapter we examine the three stories separately to see how they are similar or different. Did the narrator know the earlier account and expand it? Also, which of the three stories is the original one?

A. ABRAHAM IN EGYPT (GEN 12)

There was a famine, and as a result, Abraham was forced to go down to Egypt. Before entering Egypt, Abraham told his wife Sarah to say that she was his sister. Sarah was a beautiful woman and, being his wife, could conceivably endanger his life. Abraham and Sarah acted here as a brother and sister. This means that Abraham acted as her guardian so that he would be treated well on her account. The plan was put into motion and it succeeded. When Abraham entered Egypt, the Egyptians saw how beautiful Sarah was and took her into Pharaoh's palace. Because of Sarah, Abraham received sheep, oxen, asses, male and female slaves, she-asses, and camels. Meanwhile, God intervened, inflicting Pharaoh and his household with mighty plagues because of Sarah. Pharaoh summoned Abraham to his palace and complained to him: "What is this you have done to me! Why did you not tell me that she was your wife? Why did you say, 'She is my sister,' so that I took her as my wife?" (Gen 12:19). Pharaoh ordered Abraham to take his wife and leave. He expelled him and his wife and all that he possessed.

From a structural point of view, the story is a self-contained unit.[6] The problem that the patriarch faced is mentioned in verse 10. A plan was put into motion in verses 11–13, and its subsequent implementation and

---

3. Ibid., 105.
4. Koch, *Growth of the Biblical Tradition*, 111–32.
5. Van Seters, *Abraham in History and Tradition*, 167–91; Westermann, *Genesis 12–36*, 161–62; 318–20.
6. Van Seters, *Abraham in History and Tradition*, 169.

resulting complications are found in verses 14–16. The divine intervention and the outcome are mentioned in verses 17–20. This unit of this story has no link to the previous story or the story that follows it. Lot, Abraham's nephew who appeared in verses 4–5, does not appear in our story but would appear later in chapter 13. As for this story unit, Gunkel pointed to a mixture of worldly and religious motifs that existed at that time. According to him, the legend celebrates the cleverness of the patriarch, the beautiful matriarch, and the ever-faithful God.[7] In addition, it contains pleasure due to the misfortune of Pharaoh.

Some questions need to be asked. Did Pharaoh have a sexual relationship with Sarah? Why is the king punished, even though he did not know that Sarah was Abraham's wife? How did Pharaoh realize the plague was because he abducted Sarah? Was Abraham a liar when he claimed that Sarah was his sister? Was it moral for Abraham to accept gifts from Pharaoh when Sarah was abducted? As we shall see below, all of these questions are answered indirectly in chapter 20 where the narrative displays moral and theological issues.[8]

B. ABRAHAM IN GERAR (GEN 20)

Now this story takes place in Gerar. There is no mention of famine in the land so why did Abraham have to leave his place of habitat? No reason is given for Abraham's travels from the oasis of Kadesh and Shur to Gerar. In addition, the text does not suggest that Abraham was facing danger. Without any background or preparation, there is a statement that Abraham said of his wife Sarah, "She is my sister" (v. 2). This declaration by Abraham is explained later in verse 11. Meanwhile, we are told that Abimelech, the king of Gerar, took Sarah to his harem. There is no motive given for why he took her. At that time, the matriarch was nearly ninety years old. Van Seters pointed out that the current account is double in length than version A. Hence, the minimal details in verse 2 can be explained because version A was known already. Therefore, there was no need to recount the whole story again.[9] Indeed in verse 13 Abraham said, "So when God made me wander from my father's house, I said to her, 'Let this be the kindness that you shall do me: whatever place we come to, say there of me: He is my brother.'" This really shows that it was not a one-time incident, but a general

---

7. Gunkel, *Genesis*, 224.
8. Alexander, "Wife/Sister Incidents?," 147.
9. Van Seters, *Abraham in History and Tradition*, 171.

practice. Furthermore, the mention of God taking him from his birthplace brings us back to chapter 12.

The questions that we raised in version A—Why did God punish Pharaoh when he did not know that Sarah was Abraham's wife? And how did the king know that God was angry with him?—find their answers in version B (20:3–7). God appeared to Abimelech in a dream at night. In the dream, God warned Abimelech and told him, "You are to die because of the woman that you have taken, for she is a married woman" (v. 3). Abimelech defended himself; he did not have sexual relations with Sarah and he did not approach her. This is significant because the punishment for a person who has lain with someone's wife was the death penalty (Deut 22:22). Abraham deceived him when he said, "She is my sister," and Sarah said that Abraham was her brother. These alleged words by Sarah were not recorded earlier. Abimelech ends his response to God by saying that he had no evil intentions but that he acted with sincerity and innocence. In his response, God agrees with Abimelech: "I knew that you did this with a blameless heart," (v. 6) and He further told him that He prevented the violation of Sarah. Adultery is viewed as a sin against God. How God prevented Abimelech from approaching Sarah is not stated. God ordered Abimelech to return Sarah to Abraham. Interestingly, Abraham is not mentioned by name, but only as the husband of the woman who was taken by Abimelech. He is also referred to as "the man," and a "prophet," perhaps to indicate the distance between Abraham and Abimelech.

God's warning is concise and unambiguous. It is phrased in the present tense, as was noted by Sforno, who paraphrased it as, "You are going to succumb to a disease that will begin with you because the Lord has closed fast . . ." Indeed, the chapter concludes with the report that the Lord healed Abimelech and his wife and his slave girls (v. 17). On the surface, the text seems to be speaking of infertility, but Shadal (S. D. Luzzatto, 1800–1865) believed that the reference was about some sort of venereal disease that prevented the king from having sexual relations with his wife and concubines. After Abraham prayed on their behalf, the king and his wives were cured and the latter could give birth.

The need for Abraham to intercede is somewhat strange, because Abimelech himself conducts a dialogue with the Lord. Why, then, did Abraham have to pray for the king? We can only note the tradition ascribed to various prophets—Moses (Num 12:13), Elijah (1 Kgs 17:20– 22), and Elisha (2 Kgs 4:33–35)—and their ability to make supplication and heal others.

God's appearance to Abimelech resembles a judicial proceeding. There are several stages in the process: the indictment (v. 3), the accused's presentation of his defense (vv. 4–5), and acceptance of his argument and reversal of the original verdict (vv. 6–7). Although the sin Abimelech was to be punished for was adultery, even before he answered God the text emphasizes the euphemism "approached," that Abimelech had not yet had sexual relations with Sarah.[10] Answering God as if he is conversing with his own deity, he asks: "O Lord, will You slay people even though innocent?" (Gen 20:4). Interestingly, this question about the nature of divine justice echoes Abraham's with regard to the impending doom of the Sodomites (Gen 18:23). Then shifting the blame to Abraham, who misled him—"She is my sister"—and Sarah, who corroborated this statement—"He is my brother"—Abimelech goes on to argue that he had not known that Sarah was a married woman. The Lord accepts Abimelech's defense and tells him that he had in fact been aware of his innocence.

The exchange between God and Abimelech is in the form of a dream. Such a dream, dealing with past events, is rare, since dreams are usually future oriented. But the Lord's warning to Abimelech is in fact meant to keep him from sinning. He instructs Abimelech as to what he must do to clear his name—return Sarah to Abraham. Then God repeats his earlier warning ("You are about to die," v. 3); here, however, the Lord says to him: "You will surely die." The duplication מות תמות *môt tāmût* emphasizes the gravity of God's warning. It applies not only to Abimelech, but also to everything that belongs to him. "Know that you shall die, you and all that are yours" (Gen 20:7).[11] Thus, the dream is based upon two warnings, supplemented by instructions as to how the admonished one can purge himself of guilt.

In response to God's appearance in his dream, Abimelech acts without hesitation to do precisely as he was instructed. First thing in the morning, he summons all his servants, who are "greatly frightened" (Gen 20:8) when he tells them about the dream. The Lord has punished Abimelech because of his "great sin," namely adultery. The same idiom is found in Egyptian documents, as well as in Akkadian documents from Ugarit: "That woman has sinned a great sin against you," which evidently alludes to adultery.[12]

---

10. The root קרב k. r. b. frequently has a sexual connotation in the Bible. See Lev 18:6; 14:19; Deut 22:14; and Isa 8:3.

11. In a similar vein, the entire people are punished for David's sin (2 Sam 24:15).

12. *PRU* IV, 139–40; Rabinowitz, "'Great Sin,'" 73; Moran, "Scandal of the 'Great Sin,'" 280–81; Milgrom, *Cult and Conscience*, 132–33.

Abimelech acts at once to compensate Abraham for the damage to Sarah's reputation, giving him sheep, cattle, and slaves. The paired verbs "took" and "gave" constitute a hendiadys expressing the actions of making a donation. This idiom is common in Hittite and Ugaritic gifting documents.[13] Sarah also receives financial compensation for the slight to her reputation. As Samuel ben Meir (Rashbam, c.1080–c. 1174) states, it is so "the people will not look at you disparagingly and say, 'Abimelech treated this woman wantonly,' because everyone knew that he took her in an honorable way and returned her against his will." The financial compensation to Sarah is referred to as "a covering of the eyes," that is, a ransom payment to cover over guilt.[14] In the Middle Assyrian Laws (Tablet A, section 22), we find that if a man takes a married woman on a business trip and does not know that she is married he must take an oath to this effect and give two ingots of tin to her husband.[15]

C. ISAAC IN GERAR (GEN 26)

Later, like his father Abraham, Isaac experiences famine, and thus sets out for Egypt. Along the way he makes a stop, visiting Abimelech, the king of the Philistines at Gerar. This opening statement indicates that the narrator is familiar with accounts A and B and combined elements from both stories. The mention of the famine recalls Abraham's migration to Egypt in version A. Going to Abimelech and staying in Gerar reminds us of version B. At Gerar, God appeared to him and barred him from migrating to Egypt, and instead ordered him to stay at Gerar. In addition, God reaffirms to Isaac the covenant he had made with his father Abraham. He promised him "all these lands" and numerous descendants. The usage of the plural form in the Hebrew word "lands" is unusual and it evidently refers to neighboring groups in the territories of Sidon, Tyre, Byblos, Hermon, Lebanon, and the land of the Philistines.[16]

13. Labuschagne, "našû-nadānu Formula," 176–80.

14. The literal sense of בסות עינים *kesût 'ênayim* is "mask that covers the eyes." It should be compared to two similar expressions, the סתר פנים *sātar pānîm* (facemask) worn by an adulterer to conceal his identity (Job 24:15) and the מסוה *masweh* (veil) that Moses places over his face to block the light radiating from it (Exod 34:34). In the present verse, however, בסות עינים *kesût 'ênayim* should not be understood literally, but as an idiom. See also Levine, *In the Presence*, 60n18.

15. Driver and Miles, *Assyrian Laws*, 392, no.2:105–11; Cardascia, *Les lois assyriennes*, 138–41.

16. Sarna, *JPS Torah Commentary: Genesis*, 183.

ISAAC

While staying in Gerar the men of the place inquire about Rebekah. There was no threat to the matriarch, but Isaac felt threatened. Isaac was afraid to say that Rebekah was his wife because the Gerarites would kill him because of Rebekah's beauty. Indeed, in Genesis 24:16 she is described as very beautiful. Isaac is afraid to lose his wife and perhaps his own life. Thus, he resorts to deception and says she is his sister. He assures his own safety, but not hers. He emulates his father Abraham who also used deception when he stayed in Gerar. Verse 7, which describes the events that took place in Gerar, is a reminder of story B: "When the men of the place asked him about his wife, he said, 'She is my sister,' for he was afraid to say, 'my wife' thinking, 'The men of the place might kill me on account of Rebekah, for she is beautiful.'" Isaac's words "She is my sister" are the same words that his father Abraham used (20:2). The element of fear because of Rebekah's beauty has its parallel in 20:11: "surely there is no fear of god in this place, and they will kill me because of my wife."

Isaac stayed in Gerar a long time, which shows that he and his wife Rebekah did not face any danger and that his fears were unfounded. One day, by chance, Abimelech discovered the true nature of Isaac and Rebekah's relationship. Looking through his palace window, he saw Isaac fondling his wife Rebekah (v. 8). The king immediately sent for Isaac and rebuked him; he wanted to know the motive for Isaac's action: "So she is your wife! Why then did you say: 'She is my sister'" (v. 9)? Abimelech repeated here the same words of Isaac from verse 7. In his response, Isaac also, with some modification, repeated his previous thoughts: "Because I thought I might lose my life on account of her" (v. 9). Abimelech continued and accused Isaac: "What have you done to us!" (v. 10). As noted above, the king uses the same words that appeared in story B, "What have you done to us?" (20:9). He was afraid that one of his people might have lain with Isaac's wife, and thus harm could be done to the whole city. Abimelech shows that he is a God-fearing man. He issues a royal decree stating that any man who touches Isaac and his wife will be put to death. Gunkel raises the question: Why did Abimelech use such a forceful statement, since no one considered harming Isaac? Therefore, according to him, "The narrator had other recensions in view where such harm has, indeed, taken place."[17]

As the reader recalls in chapter 25, we read of the birth of Jacob and Esau. Here, on the other hand, there is no mention of the children at all. Isaac and Rebekah appear not to have any children, which contradicts both

17. Gunkel, *Genesis*, 223.

the previous chapter and the following one. If they already had children, no one in Gerar would have believed that they are brother and sister.[18] Hence, it appears that we have an independent narrative inserted in the wrong spot. The stories do not follow a chronological order.

COMPARISON OF STORY A AND B

Story A starts with famine, which was the main reason for the patriarch to go down to Egypt. In story B there is no explanation for why Abraham went to Gerar. In A, Abraham passes his wife off as his sister because Sarah is a beautiful woman and he is afraid that the Egyptians will kill him and let her live. If she would say that she is his sister both of them would stay alive. In story B, on the other hand, there is no explanation why Abraham ordered his wife Sarah to say that she is his sister, and not a single word about her beauty. It is only later in verse 11 that Abraham explains why he passed his wife off as his sister: "Surely there is no fear of God in this place, and they will kill me because of my wife." In story A, as Abraham predicted, Pharaoh's courtiers see how beautiful Sarah is and take her into the king's palace. Because of Sarah, the king gives Abraham presents when he takes Sarah. In story B, Sarah is taken to Abimelech and there is no mention of gifts. The gifts are lavished on Abraham when Abimelech sends Sarah back to him and are meant as compensation. In addition, Abraham is not expelled from Gerar; rather, the king gives him permission to stay in his territory: "Here, my land is before you; settle wherever you please" (20:15). The fact that Abraham received gifts and the permission to stay in the land shows that the king accepted the patriarch's explanations. It appears as though the king is the guilty party and not Abraham. In story A, on the other hand, after Pharaoh finds out that Abraham deceived him, he sent him away from his territory; he expelled him. Here Abraham is the guilty party and not Pharaoh. According to Van Seters, the relationship between Abraham and King Abimelech is reversed from story A "in order to give moral stature to the patriarch."[19]

In story A, Abraham does not respond to the king's accusation. He does not make any attempt to clear himself, which can be interpreted as an admission of guilt. In story B, he defends himself by saying that he did not expect to find "the fear of God in this place." In other words, he did not

18. Koch, *Growth of the Biblical Tradition*, 118.
19. Van Seters, *Abraham in History and Tradition*, 175.

believe that a high code of ethical behavior was part of the fabric of the city. However according to verse 8, King Abimelech and his people were greatly frightened. Abraham further explains that he does not see any wrong in his behavior since Sarah indeed is his sister. She is his father's daughter but not of the same mother; she is a half-sister. As noted in chapter 2, marriage within the family, endogamy, was commonly practiced among the patriarchs. It was only later that this practice was forbidden, which points to the antiquity of our story.

The comparison between stories A and B shows that story B has several features which indicate that the author of B had previous knowledge of version A. Therefore, in version B there is no rationale for Abraham going to Gerar, nor is there any explanation for Abraham's plan. We are simply told that Abraham said that Sarah is his sister. It is not clear why Abimelech sent for Sarah to be brought to his palace. However, in version A we were told already that Sarah was a beautiful woman, which explains the monarch's action. Indeed, some of the laconic description in version B shows that the author was expecting the reader to be familiar with the events narrated in version A (12:11–15). Indeed, version B (20:2) cannot be understood without 12:11–15.[20] Furthermore, Abraham's statement in 20:13, "whatever place we come to, say there of me: He is my brother," suggests that he refers to the previous events of 12:10–13.

STORY C IN COMPARISON TO A AND B

According to Van Seters, when we examine version C, it is not an independent folk tale, but rather a "further version of both stories A and B."[21] It is a story that comes to show the parallels between the lives of Isaac and Abraham. It is missing moral and theological questions regarding the wife-sister deception. Clearly it is "an artificial literary tradition about Isaac based directly on the traditions of Abraham."[22]

Traveling: According to version A, Abraham travels to Egypt to the land of Pharaoh. In version B, Abraham travels to Gerar, and in version C it is Isaac who travels to Gerar. Abimelech and Pharaoh are the counterheroes. Abimelech and Gerar are mentioned twice, while Pharaoh only once. Hence, it is more logical to transfer a story about a less-important king and

---

20. Alexander, "Wife/Sister Incidents?," 147.
21. Van Seters, *Abraham in History and Tradition*, 177.
22. Ibid., 183.

a small country to a well-known king and country such as Egypt, rather than the other way around.[23]

Reasoning for the deception: In version A, we are told that Sarah is a beautiful woman. Thus, to save his life, Abraham asks her to lie and say that she is his sister. In version B, there is no mention of Sarah's beauty; Abraham passes Sarah off as his sister (v. 2) and asks her to lie (v. 13). It is only after Abimelech finds out the truth in a dream and rebukes Abraham that the patriarch explains his behavior. Accordingly, there is no fear of God in the place and he is afraid he will be killed because of his wife. Furthermore, Abraham gives an answer by explaining that she is indeed his sister from his father's side. In other words, she is a half-sister. It appears version B is very sensitive to the plausibility of the relationship between Abimelech and Sarah where a sin might be committed, in addition to the lie that Abraham uttered. This version also explains the gifts that Abraham received, which were not a bridal price but were reparation for hurting Sarah's honor. We can see that version B contains religious and moral aspects that were missing from version A. Version C is very similar to A; we read that Rebekah is very beautiful. Thus, Isaac fears for his life so he passes his wife Rebekah off as his sister. This explanation is repeated after Abimelech rebukes Isaac: "Because I thought I might lose my life on account of her" (26:9).

Discovery of the deception: In version A, there is no explanation how Pharaoh discovers that Sarah is Abraham's wife. Also, the text does not say that he approaches her. In version B, God tells Abimelech in a dream that Sarah is a married woman. God warns him not to touch Sarah, and he indeed does not come close to her. In version C, the discovery that Rebekah is Isaac's wife is by chance. It is noteworthy that the language used by the monarch upon discovering the truth is similar:

- What is this you have done to me? (Gen 12:18)
- What have you done to us? (Gen 20:9)
- What is this you have done to us? (Gen 26:10)

Punishment: In version A, the Lord afflicted Pharaoh and his household with mighty plagues. In version B, there are no plagues, but there is a threat of death. In version C, there are no plagues and no threat since the king discovered that Rebekah was Isaac's wife.

---

23. Koch, *Growth of the Biblical Tradition*, 125.

Adultery: In version A, Pharaoh takes Sarah into his court. What happens between them is not explicitly stated but one can imagine. In version B, we read several times that nothing offensive takes place because God prevents it. In version C, the narrator removes any possibility of something taking place but suggests that someone could have desired the matriarch. Since version A contains *offensive things*, it is the most *morally offensive* which is not the case with versions B and C.

Acceptance of guilt: In version A, Pharaoh complains that Abraham misled him, but there is not a single word about the sin that was committed or about to be committed. In version B, Abimelech complains about the great sin that Abraham has caused him and his kingdom. He asks him to explain the purpose of misleading him. In response, Abraham apologizes, saying he thought there was no fear of God at this place. In version C, there is a development regarding sin. The king could commit a sin and the whole community would have been subject to punishment.

Presents and Wealth: According to version A, Pharaoh gives Abraham presents when he takes Sarah to his house, which makes it appear as though he purchases Sarah. The story starts with Abraham having little or no wealth and ends with Abraham being a wealthy man. In version B, Abraham is already a rich man; as is stated in Genesis 13:2, "Now Abraham was very rich in cattle, in silver, and in gold." The presents he receives are to compensate Abraham for the fact that Sarah is taken to Abimelech's house; the presents are a form of reparation. In version C, there is no harm done to Rebekah, thus there is no reason for gifts. Nevertheless, after the event, Isaac receives blessings from God, not men: "The Lord blessed him, and the man grew richer and richer until he was very wealthy: he acquired flocks and herds, and a large household" (Gen 26:12–13).

Protection: In version A, God inflicts Pharaoh with plagues, preventing him from touching Sarah. In version B, God warns Abimelech in a dream not to touch Sarah. In version C, it is Abimelech himself who threatens his people with the death penalty if Rebekah is touched. God's protection is missing here; it only appears in the background (Gen 26:3). Since no evil occurs there is no need for God's involvement. The more detailed versions (A and B) contain an explanation for divine revelation. Version C is a simple story where the king perceives the truth by himself. There is no need for divine intervention, which suggests it was the original story.[24]

---

24. Lutz, "Isaac Tradition," 141.

ISAAC'S WIFE-SISTER

Expulsion: In version A, Pharaoh provides guards to accompany the patriarch's departure of his country. In version B, Abraham can stay in Gerar. In version C, Isaac can stay, but later the king asks him to leave: "Go away from us, for you have become far too big for us" (26:16). Isaac is sent away because of jealousy; he has become too rich.

STORY REPETITION

Repetition is a well-known technique that was used by the biblical narrator and is found in the literature of the ancient world. By repeating stories and adding or subtracting details, the narrator could stress a point. The patriarchs were fallible human beings. There is no attempt to idealize them. They are described with all their faults and weakness, with stories portraying simple people who are living their daily lives. The audience was familiar already with the stories and their outcome and enjoyed hearing the stories repeatedly. When the author wanted to stress a point, he would repeat the story. Therefore, when Pharaoh had a dream about the seven cows, it was followed by a second dream of seven ears of grain. Joseph, while interpreting Pharaoh's dream, said: "Pharaoh's dreams are one and the same: God has told Pharaoh what He is about to do" (Gen 41:25). In other words, every time the author wanted to emphasize a point, he would repeat the story. He would alter and change some of the story motifs, but preserved its core by using similar words and expressions.

Deception was a way of life in the ancient world and in this respect the Hebrews were no different from other people. In the Jacob cycle, for example, trickery and deceptions are one of the main motifs. All protagonists take part and play a role in deception. Similarly, in Greek literature, humans and gods deceive each other. Athena dressed herself up as an old man. Penelope lied about Laertes' magically shrinking shroud. Odysseus was the king of liars. As for the gods, they too deceived all the time. The aim of these deceptions was to gain the advantage of being in control, to have the upper hand. However, as we read in the Ten Commandments (Exod 20:7), in the Hebrew Bible, with its high moral standard, did not approve of this kind of trickery. Surprisingly, Abraham and Isaac are not punished for their deception. In fact, God protects them. God—who chose Abraham, made promises to him, watched over him and his wife, and rescued them from danger—does the same with Isaac.

ISAAC

The stories were also foreshadowing future events. Hence, the story about Abraham and Sarah's migration to Egypt is very similar to the story of the Israelites' descent to Egypt and the Exodus.[25] This is not limited to subject matter but also to the usage of language. Abraham went to Egypt because of the famine (Gen 12:10); later, the famine was again the reason Israelites went down to Egypt (43:1). In both incidents, the famine is described as severe. The fear that Abraham expressed "they will kill me and let you live" (12:12) is a reminder of "if it is a boy, kill him; if it is a girl, let her live" (Exod 1:16). Taking Sarah to Pharaoh's harem is parallel to the taking of the Israelites into slavery. The presents that Abraham received in Egypt (Gen 12:16), and the mention of it when he left Egypt ("cattle, silver, and gold," 13:2), are like the silver and gold the Israelites received from the Egyptians when they left Egypt (Exod 3:21–22; 11:2–3; 12:35–36). God interceded in both stories and inflicted plagues on the Egyptians (Gen 12:17; Exod 11:1). These parallels are not coincidence, but further proof of the author's desire to show the similarities between the stories.[26]

Similarly, foreshadowing future events is also found in Abraham and Sarah's story in Egypt and Gerar. These stories serve as background for the Isaac and Rebekah story in Gerar. The author creates a story here, which encompasses elements from the previous stories in Genesis. In spite of all the troubles with the Egyptians and the Philistines, God protected Abraham. Similarly, he would later protect his descendants, as we read in the stories of the Exodus and the return of the Ark (1 Sam 6). In other words, this is a message of faith which the author conveyed so the Israelites could be sure God would come to their aid in times of need.[27]

Expansion is found in the story of Isaac and Rebekah in Gerar. The author referred here to Isaac and Rebekah instead of Abraham and Sarah. He used motifs that were found in stories A and B. The major difference is that in story C God is not intervening directly, but he is behind the scenes. The guiding hand of God is felt. The way that God helped the patriarchs in the past was a testimony for the future, that God would guide and protect the Israelites.

It is noteworthy that the stories about the patriarchs Abraham, Isaac, and Jacob have recurrent elements. The stories are repeated three times, which confirms the idea of a chosen nation that would spring up from the

---

25. Cassuto, "Quaestio," 258.
26. Ibid., 258–59.
27. Ibid., 261.

three patriarchs. Each of the patriarchs left his family: Abraham from his brother Nahor and later from his nephew Lot; Isaac from Ishmael; and Jacob from Esau. Each of the patriarchs received the promise of the land and many descendants. Each married women from Aram Naharaim and had to wait for a long period for the birth of an heir. During their lives, they left their place of habitat several times. They had to move because of the famine. In their new living place, they faced danger and God protected them. They made covenants with the Canaanites and the Philistines, in addition to maintaining ownership of part of the land of Israel.[28]

On the other hand, there are stories that feature repeated motifs between two patriarchs. Therefore, Abraham and Jacob both migrated from Aram Naharaim. Their journeys in the land of Canaan follow the same route. They took concubines because of the barrenness of their wives. Counterparts are also found in the Isaac and Jacob stories: the searches for wives for Isaac and Jacob took place in Aram Naharaim; as did the blessing of a son by passing over the older son in favor of the younger. Sometimes the repetition appears in the next generation. Isaac had twins, and later it is Judah, Jacob's son, who has twins. As in the Isaac story, where the younger twin tries to get out from his mother's womb first, so it is in Judah's story. There are incidents where repetition is recorded in the life of the patriarch himself. Hence, Abraham migrated twice: first to Egypt, then to Gerar. So too with Jacob, who migrated to Aram Naharaim and then to Egypt. Twice Jacob took concubines because of the barrenness of his wives. All these repetitions and parallel stories show us that this is a pattern that exists in the patriarchal narrative. What we have here is one story about a patriarch who faced danger in a foreign land and in order to avert the danger passed his wife off as his sister. This is not a patchwork of different sources; rather, by repeating the stories and making changes, the author tried to display the similarities and differences between the patriarchs.[29]

In conclusion, the danger that the matriarchs faced in foreign territory is described in the book of Genesis three times. Version A is Sarah in the house of Pharaoh (ch. 12); version B is Sarah in the house of Abimelech (ch. 20); and version C is Rebekah in the house of Abimelech (ch. 26). An examination of these stories shows that there are progressive developments. Story B has several features which indicate the author of B had previous knowledge of version A. Furthermore, in version B we find answers

28. Ibid., 263.
29. Ibid., 262-64.

Isaac

to some of the questions that were left open in version A. In version C, we find elements from both stories A and B. During the course of its inclusion within the book of Genesis, story C was altered in order to show the parallels between the lives of Abraham and Isaac. However, it is missing the moral and theological questions regarding the wife-sister deception. It is clearly an artificial literary tradition about Isaac based directly on the traditions of Abraham. Probably during the process of their incorporation into the book of Genesis the three accounts were modified in light of each other. Examination of the three versions shows that they are organized chronologically. Version A is the most ancient one. Version B appeared later and is based on version A. Version C is the most recent based on the previous two.

The next and last chapter will examine Isaac's blessing that he gave to his two sons, Esau and Jacob. In addition, we will describe the death of Isaac.

8

Isaac and His Sons

Isaac was sixty years old when his twins were born—twenty years after marrying Rebekah,[1] whose age, on the other hand, is never mentioned. We are only told that she is a barren woman. Rebekah, like Sarah, is barren, as is Rachel, Jacob's future wife. In other words, all of the matriarchs were barren. This theme is repeated later with the mothers of Samson and Samuel. Another motif that is common to these stories is Yahweh's power to open the womb. By opening the womb of barren women, God shows his power and signals the arrival of the special child. According to Gunkel: "A long infertility of the mother before the birth of the child is a favored legend motif. How passionately the child is desired! The child is a gift of God from the very beginning. It is no wonder that so much becomes of him later."[2] In this chapter we examine the birth of Isaac's twin sons, Jacob and Esau, with an explanation of what stands behind this story. Does it come to explain the relationship between the two brothers? Or maybe the stories were created in order to explain the complex relationship between Israel and Edom in the later periods? Isaac felt that he was going to die, therefore he sent his son Esau to hunt for him, so he could then bless him. However, this plan failed because Jacob deceived his old and blind father and also tricked his brother. Jacob stole the blessing from Esau. Why did Jacob act in this manner and what was he to gain by his deception? In addition, the blessing

---

1. Isaac was forty years old when he married Rebekah. According to the Talmud, if one is not married by twenty he is cursed by God. See *b. Sanh.* 76b.
2. Gunkel, *Genesis*, 288.

Isaac

that Isaac bestowed on his sons will be examined to see how different the blessings are. Finally, in the last part of the chapter, we will study the subject of Isaac's death.

THE BIRTH OF TWINS

Like other heroes in the biblical narrative, this one also requires divine intervention. Isaac, although described as a passive man who was controlled by his father and manipulated by his wife, finally acts. He takes the initiative and implores God on behalf of his wife. Isaac prays to God to open his wife's womb. His prayers were answered and his wife Rebekah conceives. In contrast to Abraham and Sarah who resorted to concubinage, Isaac and Rebekah put their trust in God. The word that describes Isaac's prayers עתר *ātar*, is the same word that was used by Manoah, Samson's father, before God removed the barrenness from his wife. How much time passed between Isaac's prayers and God answering his prayers, we are not told. The fact that God responded to his prayers shows how powerful his prayers were.

Isaac's prayers were answered and Rebekah became pregnant with not one, but two sons. Rebekah had a difficult pregnancy; the children struggled in her womb, and she suffered from "quickening," constant movements of the fetuses. To describe the movements of the twins, the Bible uses the verb ויתרצצו *va-yitrotestsu*, which means "they crushed, thrust one another" (Gen 25:22). This description foreshadows the future relationship between the nation of Israel and Edom, represented by these two sons. The pregnancy was so difficult that Rebekah says: "If so, why do I exist?" (Gen 25:22). In other words, there is no point to life. A similar thought is expressed later by Rebekah after the deception episode: "What good will life be to me?" (27:46). Because of her difficult pregnancy, Rebekah went to inquire of the Lord. The Hebrew word for "inquire" is a technical term for inquiring of oracles. The Bible does not tell what kind of method she used. In the ancient world, people usually went to a temple or to a prophet. However, in the patriarchal period there are no cultic personnel nor a specific shrine. It was suggested that because the matriarch lived in Beer-lahai-roi, where earlier Hagar received the divine announcement about the birth of her son, Rebekah possibly went to the same site.[3] No particular details are given about this consultation because they probably were not important; instead the message itself is described.

---

3. Sarna, *JPS Torah Commentary: Genesis*, 179.

Isaac and His Sons

The divine name Yahweh appears both in the inquiry as well as in the oracle. The mention of the name Yahweh is not coincidental; it came to remove any suspicion of Rebekah being engaged in a pagan cultic rite. We have to remember that she belonged to a family of idol worshippers. The oracle that Rebekah received from God included a prophetic message stating that she would have twins where the older shall serve the younger:

> "Two nations are in your womb.
> Two separate peoples shall issue from your body;
> One people shall be mightier than the other
> And the older shall serve the younger." (Gen 25:23)

This oracle was very significant because it justified Rebekah's later role in the deception of her husband Isaac. More importantly, it shows that Jacob was the true heir to the covenant with Abraham and Isaac. Jacob was chosen in the womb before anyone knew what would become of him. Jacob would surpass his older brother Esau. This forecasts the future of Jacob's domination of Esau and Israel's subjugation of Edom. The oracle refers to the future relationship between the Israelites and the Edomites. Each of the boys will become a progenitor of a separate nation. In reality, this oracle started to be fulfilled during the lifetime of the brothers when Jacob gained the upper hand. First, Esau relinquished his birthright to Jacob in exchange for a meal (25:29–34), and then Esau lost the patriarchal blessing (Gen 27). In the Hebrew Bible, we have many examples of the younger brother who replaces his older brother. Thus, we read of Isaac and Ishmael, Zerah and Pertz, Ephraim and Manasseh, David and his older brothers, as well as Solomon and Adonijah.

Historically speaking, the Edomites became a settled kingdom before Israel. Esau (Edom) was the older brother. The Israelites (the younger) subjugated the Edomites (the older) in the tenth century BCE during the time of David: "and all the Edomites became David's servants" (2 Sam 8:14). Later, however, this would change, as mentioned in Isaac's blessing to Esau: "But when you grow restive, you shall break his yoke from your neck" (Gen 27:40). This reference is to the reign of King Jehoram in the mid-ninth century when Edom successfully revolted and attained its independence (2 Kgs 8:20–22). Sixty years later, Amaziah defeated ten thousand Edomites and subdued them. He defeated the Edomites, captured Sela in the battle, renamed it Joktheel, and annexed it to Judah (2 Kgs 14:7; 2 Chr 25:11–12). The Edomites regained their freedom again during the reign of Ahaz (735–715 BCE) who was pressured by Rezin, king of Aram (2 Kgs 16:6). Judah, as a result, was forced to give Elath to the Edomites who settled there.

The stories about Jacob and Esau were probably created in order to explain the complex relationship between Israel and Edom in later periods. The fact that Jacob and Esau were kin is attested to in numerous biblical texts. In Deuteronomy 23:8, Moses commands: "Do not abhor the Edomite, for he is your brother." This verse distinguishes between the Edomites and other nations such as the Ammonites and the Moabites, who are condemned in the previous verse. In the song of Deborah, which is considered to be one of the oldest pieces of Hebrew poetry, God is described as marching from the plains of Edom to save his people. Evidently, the biblical texts came to convey the idea of the existing linkage between Israel and Edom. Indeed, a place by the name *Yahwi* was found in the Egyptian inscription from Seir dating to the late Bronze Age.[4] This shows that Yahweh was already an important god in Edom, further indicating the connections between Israel and Edom. Originally, Jacob and Esau were heads of tribal clans. The biblical story that describes them as brothers came to illustrate the close connections between the two people. They spoke similar dialects and also shared a cultural tie, which is why the narrative in Genesis suggests that they were twins. The hostile relationship between Edom and Israel was attributed to an earlier period, back to the birth of the brothers. The way the brothers fought was later emulated by Israel and Edom.

There are scholars who reject the idea that the relationship between Jacob and Esau reflects the future relationship between Israel and Edom. Gunkel, for example, says that we don't know anything about Esau and Jacob, and the traditions of Jacob and Esau as brothers is a later traditional story. He points to the fact that many features of the story are not applicable to Israel and Edom: "in the legend Jacob is not disposed to war; in history Israel conquered Edom in war; in the legend Esau is stupid, in history he is famous for his wisdom."[5] Furthermore, Esau's name does not have much in common with the name Edom, which has a reputation of wisdom in the Hebrew Bible. Gunkel maintains that the conflict of the two brothers is a reflection of the ascent of herders over hunters in ancient Palestine.[6] Noth

---

4. Giveon, *Les Bédouins Shosou*, 26–28. On the Midianite hypothesis, see de Vaux, *Early History of Israel*, 330–38.

5. Gunkel, *Legends of Genesis*, 24.

6. Ibid., 24–26.

followed Gunkel's line of thinking and suggested that the stories about Jacob and Esau were told in the circles of herdsman who enjoyed telling them. The stories were originated among the East Jordanian Ephraimites in the land of Gilead. The stories represent a time when in Gilead, the huntsman, who was the first and the older, was replaced by the younger herdsman. In this tradition, Esau represents an unknown ethnic group or "a type of huntsman in contrast to Jacob, who represents the herdsman."[7] According to him, the main object of the Jacob-Esau story is to exhibit that the herdsman receives preference over the huntsman. The herdsman thinks he is entitled to receive preference, and he achieves it by the stupidity of the huntsman and by his own cleverness and craftiness.[8] However, nowhere in the earlier stories of Jacob and Esau is Jacob described as a herdsman. Furthermore, the blessing that he receives from his father suits a farmer better.[9] Hendel does not accept the idea that the stories about Jacob and Esau originally represent the relationship between Israel and Edom, and no definitive view can be determined.[10] According to him, at some point, Jacob and Esau: "were identified as eponymous ancestors of political groups, and that neither the narrative of the two brothers nor the history of the two nations can be discerned with any clarity through the other."[11] Later, he modified his position, suggesting that the Jacob and Esau story is representative of the conflict between civilizations and nature. Hence, Genesis 25 and 27 exhibit contrasts between Jacob and Esau. Here, Jacob is identified with civilization while Esau is wild and uncivilized.[12] Indeed, the relationship between Jacob and Esau is also an expression of cultural and ethnic self-definition, but this was not the intent of the story. The story comes to show how the weaker, smaller brother successfully dominated his older brother.[13]

THE DECEPTION OF ESAU

The first two episodes portray Jacob in a negative light (Gen 25:27— 34:27). In the first story, he takes advantage of his hungry brother. Jacob is cooking

---

7. Noth, *History of Pentateuchal Traditions*, 96–97.
8. Ibid., 97.
9. Kugel, *How to Read the Bible*, 710n6.
10. Hendel, *Epic of the Patriarch*, 115.
11. Ibid.
12. McCarter and Hendel, "Patriarchal Age," 27.
13. Kugel, *How to Read the Bible*, 710n6.

a stew at home, which was an important part of the daily diet, mainly because of its nutritional benefit. The stew was made of lentils or beans, which were softened during cooking. This yellowish red or dark brown plant was cultivated in the ancient Near East. When Jacob served it to Esau, he added something that gave it a red color.[14]

Meanwhile, his brother Esau went to hunt but returned empty-handed, so he was famished. Since he was hungry, he asked his brother Jacob to give him some of the red stew to eat. Describing his request to eat, the Bible uses the word "gulp down." The word is a *hapax legomenon*, and Skinner says this is "a coarse expression suggesting bestial voracity."[15] Speiser refers to Esau as "an uncouth glutton."[16] In rabbinic Hebrew, the word was used for the feedings of animals.[17] We can see that from the start, the narrator portrays Esau in a negative light. Responding to his brother's request for food, Jacob answers without hesitation. Jacob wants his brother's birthright so he asks him to sell it to him. Jacob knows exactly what he wants and he pursues it with determination and resolve. Did Jacob know about the oracle that his mother received? Or did his mother tell him about it? At this stage, we don't know.

What was behind Jacob's request for the purchase of the birthright? The firstborn was held in great esteem in Israel. He was considered the first fruits of his father's strength (Gen 49:3) and dedicated to God (Exod 22:28). More importantly, when the inheritance was divided, the firstborn received a double share or twice as much as his other brothers (Deut 21:17). Was it common to sell the birthright? It appears that there are some texts from Nuzi from the fifteenth century BCE which parallel the exchange between Esau and Jacob. One text mentions a person by the name of Tupkitilla who transfers his inheritance rights for a grove to his brother Kurpazah for three sheep: "On the day they divided the grove (that lies) on the road of the town of Lumti . . . Tupkitilla shall give it to Kurpazah as his inheritance share. And Kurpazah has taken three sheep to Tupkitilla in exchange for his inheritance share."[18] It is not clear, however, if Tupkitilla is the elder brother. Was the grove the entire inheritance or just a portion? There is no mention of hunger

---

14. Elisha served a similar stew to the disciples of the prophets. After it was boiled in the pot, they were almost poisoned (2 Kgs 4:38–41).

15. Skinner, *Genesis*, 361.

16. Speiser, *Genesis*, 195.

17. Mish. *Shab.* 24:3; *b. Shab.* 155b; *b. Ḥul.* 55b, 58b.

18. Gordon, "Biblical Customs," 5.

ISAAC AND HIS SONS

by Tupkitilla or any motivation for selling the grove.[19] Nevertheless, the text from Nuzi illustrates that a brother could sell inherited property. But more importantly, it appears that Esau sold his portion and nothing else. Esau's rank is not affected by this transaction as chapter 27 shows quite clearly.[20]

The firstborn son receives a double share of his father's inheritance; therefore, it is not clear why Esau sold his birthright for almost nothing. The text further says that he despised it (Gen 25:34). In other places, the Bible calls Esau a wicked man. This idea is repeated in the book of Hebrews: "that no one be immoral and irreligious like Esau, who sold his birthright for a single meal" (12:16). It was not only the birthright that he despised, but he did not see any harm in marrying a Hittite woman, while Isaac and Rebekah thought that endogamy was important in preserving family ties. Esau sold his birthright because, at that time, Isaac was a poor man and Esau did not think much of the birthright. Still, if Isaac was poor, why did Jacob want the birthright? It is possible that the rights of the firstborn and the blessings were tied together; therefore, Jacob went to great lengths to get it. Interestingly, in the Hebrew language, there is a play on the words "first born" (*běkōrâ*) and "blessing" (*běrākâ*). What Esau lost here paved the way for a greater loss: the loss of the blessing.

What is surprising is Jacob's behavior. He took advantage of Esau and, without any shame, took from him his birthright for almost nothing. Abarbanel (Isaac ben Judah, 1437– 1508) pointed out that Jacob's behavior was immoral:

> Had Jacob been blameless and upright, how could he have dared to tell his brother to sell him his birthright for a bit of lentil porridge, since it is not worthy of a God-fearing man who turns from evil to covet something that is not his, all the more so buying from him the birthright for a contemptible price such as a bowl of lentil porridge. And if Esau is a foolish man, Jacob should have been a just man and not trick him.

THE DECEPTION OF ISAAC

Later in life, Isaac became old and blind. Old age that is accompanied by poor vision is often a sign of approaching death, yet Isaac lived many years

---

19. Van Seters, *Abraham in History and Tradition*, 92–93; Thompson, *Historicity of the Patriarchal Narratives*, 280–85; Selman, "Comparative Customs," 97, 116, 123, 135–36.

20. Tsevat, "B\u1e17khôr," 126.

afterwards. The fact that Isaac was blind is also used figuratively in the text to tell the reader that he did not know his sons. He never observed his sons in their daily pursuits. The mention of blindness is foreshadowing the future where Jacob will steal the birthright from his brother. In the story, Isaac is a victim of intrigue devised by his wife and Jacob.

At first glance it appears that Isaac preferred Esau over Jacob. He probably admired Esau for his skill as a mighty hunter. Not surprisingly, he asked him to hunt for him and prepare for him tasty game. Isaac, because of his old age, wanted to bless Esau. Since Esau was his oldest son, he wanted to practice the custom of primogeniture. Pronouncing blessings requires physical comfort, which is the result of good food and drink. According to Seforno, Isaac wanted to give Esau a chance to serve him so he would not be prejudiced on his behalf. Interestingly, from Ugarit we learn that a youth had to undergo an initiation rite into manhood that included trapping and hunting game.[21] In choosing Esau, he elected a son who was the opposite of himself. Esau represents forcefulness and action; he was a hunter, a man of the open field. Isaac, on the other hand, was a quiet, peaceful, tent-dweller. Perhaps Esau represents everything that Isaac wanted to be, thus by choosing him he fulfilled himself.

Jacob took advantage of Isaac, and he stole the blessing from his brother, Esau. Jacob masqueraded as Esau and misled his father into believing he was blessing his older son. It was immoral to deceive a blind man and a parent (Lev 19:14; Exod 21:17). Furthermore, Deuteronomy 27:18 invokes a curse on those who mislead the blind. Hence, Jacob brought a curse upon himself.

In this episode, Rebekah is the force behind Jacob; she dresses him up and pulls the strings that move him. Jacob recognized the risk that was involved in the plot. The Bible describes his actions by three verbs: "He went, he took, he brought." If the plan failed and his father Isaac discovered his identity, he would be the subject of his father's curse. Jacob agrees to his mother's plan only after his mother assured him that the curse would fall on her and not him. Rebekah is the first person who suggested being the recipient of a curse.[22] Jacob knows that a failure to act now will mean forfeiture of the blessing. In this episode, Jacob is cool and calculating; he advances his ambitions at the expense of his brother. In the end, Jacob

---

21. Watson, "Falcon Episode," 75.
22. Allen, "On Me Be the Curse," 159–72.

receives the blessing, but his victory is bittersweet because Jacob has to run away from his brother's rage.

The rabbis tried to justify Jacob's actions by attributing the blame to Rebekah. Furthermore, they felt that Isaac and Abraham fathered unworthy sons.[23] They believed that Esau could not be equal to Jacob, who was regarded as a model of virtue and righteousness.[24] Furthermore, they even said that God was helping with the deception:

> "When Esau was hunting and tying [his catch], the angel was untying and setting it free. Again the angel would set it free. And why? In order to prolong the hours until Jacob will go and do [what he needed] and goes in to his father and his father will eat and Jacob will take the blessing."[25]

Still, this does not change the reality of the biblical narrative, where Jacob appears as a conniving liar. Indeed, deception is one of Jacob's traits in his feuds with family members as well as with his foes, due to his inferior position (25:29–34; 27:20; 30:31–43; 32:14–22). Not surprisingly, the sympathy of the narrator was with Esau, and the biblical text describes him as crying bitterly. Even in the rabbinic literature, Jacob is criticized. Thus, Esau's "exceedingly great and bitter cry" (Gen 27:34) had been punished in the days of Mordecai who also wailed "with a great and bitter cry" (Esth 4:1).[26]

In the deception scene, Jacob and Isaac are the only two actors. There is great tension displayed. The reader waits to see if Jacob will succeed in his act of deception. Isaac speaks eight times while Jacob merely four. Only after Isaac says "The voice is Jacob's but the hands are Esau's," we read that Jacob speaks once and utters a single Hebrew word: "I am," (Gen 27:4). Isaac uses all his senses: hearing, touching, tasting, and smelling. It was the skin disguise that saved Jacob, he smelled and felt like Esau to Isaac. The only hurdle was his voice, he could not imitate his brother. Therefore, his father asks him, "Are you really my son Esau?" (Gen 27:24).

Soon after Jacob leaves, having received the blessing, his brother Esau then arrives. The narrative reaches another climax. The text is full of emotion. When Esau says: "I am your son, Esau, your firstborn" (v. 32), Isaac is in a state of shock: "Isaac was seized with very violent trembling" (v. 33).

23. *b. Pes. 56a*; *Gen. Rab.* 68:11.
24. *b. Mak.* 24a
25. *Tanḥ Toledot* 10.
26. *Gen. Rab.* 67:4.

He could not imagine that he was deceived. But more importantly, he could not change the blessing as it was irrevocable. Because of this, Esau did not ask his father to change the blessing but also to bless him. Isaac, without hesitation, identifies the deceiver: "Your brother came with deceit and took your blessing" (v. 35). Targum Pseudo-Jonathan and Onkelos translate here: "Your brother came in with *wisdom*." This is because they thought that Esau was unworthy of the blessing of his father. However, as mentioned above, the narrator's sympathy is with Esau. In his bitter outburst, Esau says that Jacob cheated him twice. There is the play on the name Jacob (*yaʿakov*) as deriving from *yaʿakov*, "heel." This is the second time that there is wordplay on the name Jacob. The word *yaʿakov* appears only here, and in Jeremiah 9:3(4) and in Hosea 12:4(3) as a description of Jacob's behavior. Based on the Ugaritic cognate *ʿkv*, "to deceive, impede," it was suggested that the verb means to deceive. Evidently, at this stage, Esau finally understood the meaning of Jacob's name. Using wordplay again, Esau complains that Jacob took his "birthright" (*bekhorah*) and "blessing" (*berakhah*). Still, how can Esau complain that Jacob deceived him after he himself sold his birthright to Jacob and even swore it to him?

Questions need to be raised here about Isaac's conduct as well. Didn't Isaac see that Jacob was the worthier man and Esau was unworthy of his blessing? An examination of the following chapter shows that Isaac was aware of his surroundings. He saved the real blessing for Jacob, the blessing of the Abrahamic covenant. The first blessing he gave to Jacob while thinking he was Esau. The blessing has three parts: 1) Assurance of fertility of the soil, which is described as an abundance of grain and wine; 2) Political supremacy that people will serve and bow to him; and 3) God's protection, which includes cursing and blessing. What's missing in this blessing is the lack of promises of progeny and the promise of the land. The second blessing was given to Esau. The structure of the blessing is similar to that of Jacob's. In the blessing, Isaac speaks of the fertility of the earth and the relations between brothers and nations. The blessing does not mention God nor the abundance of new grain and wine, which was already mentioned in Jacob's blessing. Since there is no abundance of grain and wine, it is believed this is why Isaac says: "by your sword you shall live" (Gen 27:40). Nevertheless, Esau's strength is restricted since "you shall serve your brother" (Gen 27:40). Hence, the blessing here is linked to the oracle Rebekah received: "the older shall serve the younger" (25:23). Not to end the blessing on a bad note, Isaac says: "But when you grow restive, you shall break his yoke from your neck" (Gen 27:40). It is believed that those words were added later. It probably refers to a later period when Edom broke Israel's yoke during the reign of King Joram (2 Kgs 8:20) or King Ahaz (2 Kgs 16:6).

The last blessing was given to Jacob. On the eve of Jacob's departure to Paddan-aram, Isaac blessed Jacob as the heir to the Abrahamic covenant. It appears that all along, his desire was to bless Jacob and to give him the most valuable of all the blessings. Hence, Isaac saved the progeny and the promise of the land for Jacob. The blessing included nationhood and national territory and many descendants. In other words, the promises that were previously given to Abraham (Gen 12:2–3, 7; 13:15, 17; 15:7–8, 18; 17:1, 6, 8, 16, 20; 22:17; 24:7) and Isaac (26:3–4, 24) are repeated here as those that were given to Jacob.

Jacob was punished severely for his acts of deception. Jacob was elected by God as it was revealed to Rebekah in the divine oracle that she received during her difficult pregnancy (Gen 25:23). Regardless, Jacob demonstrated his impatience by trying to speed up his predestined right to be Isaac's heir. For his impatience, Jacob paid heavily. Hence, when he appeared before Pharaoh and reported the years of his life, he said: "few and hard" (47:9). This description is in contrast to Abraham's life where the Scripture says that he died at "a good ripe age old and contented" (25:8), or Isaac "at a ripe old age" (35:29). The descriptions of Jacob's life as "few and hard" are an accurate description. At a young age he had to flee from the rage of his brother to stay in exile for twenty years. In Laban's house, his father-in-law took advantage of him and substituted Leah for Rachel. Furthermore, he changed his wages time after time. On his way home, he encountered a mysterious assailant, which left him with a strained hip. He was fearful of the upcoming meeting with his brother. His daughter Dinah was raped (ch 34), and his beloved wife Rachel died while giving birth (35:16–20). Joseph, the son of his beloved wife, was sold into slavery by his brothers. The brothers used an article of his clothing to deceive their father, just as Jacob had used Esau's clothes to mislead Isaac. It is clear that Jacob was condemned for his immoral behavior, with unequivocal condemnation found in the prophetic books. Hosea says that the Lord once "punished Jacob for his conduct, requited him for his deed" (12:3). And Jeremiah warns: "Beware, every man for his friend! Trust not even a brother! For every brother takes advantage, every friend is base in his dealing" (9:3).

Isaac

THE DEATH OF ISAAC

Since it was believed that a man was reunited with his ancestors, all the patriarchs and matriarchs, except for Rachel, were buried in the Cave of Machpelah, which Abraham purchased from Ephron the Hittite. The patriarchs were buried in the ancestral tomb on family-owned land. The Bible describes burial with the verb קבר *qbr*. The root *qbr* is common to all Semitic languages. "Death" and "burial" often appear together, thus we find the consecutive forms: "he died . . . and was buried." In addition, the name of the subject and the place of burial are common: "And Abraham breathed his last, dying. . . . His sons Isaac and Ishmael buried him in the cave of Machpelah" (Gen 25:8). The burial act was done by the son who carried the line of the family who received the blessing. Abraham was buried by Isaac and Ishmael in the Cave of Machpelah. Similarly, Isaac was buried by his sons, Esau and Jacob. The fact that the two brothers buried their father together signify reconciliation had taken place between the estranged brothers.

The death of Isaac is recorded in Genesis 35:27–29. The mention of Isaac's death at the end of chapter 35 does not appear in chronological order. It appears here with the mentioning of Esau to create a link to the next chapter which includes the listing of Esau's descendants. We are told that Jacob came to his father Isaac at Mamre, at Kiriath-arba (now Hebron), the place where Abraham and Isaac lived. Isaac was one hundred and eighty years old at the time of his death (Gen 35:28). According to the text, he was gathered to his kin at a ripe old age. Following death, it was believed that a man was reunited with his ancestors. This belief is expressed in the Bible by idioms such as "lie down with one's father" (Gen 47:30; Deut 31:16; 2 Sam 7:12; as well as being mentioned thirty-five times in 1 and 2 Kings and 2 Chronicles). The Torah employs a similar expression: "He was gathered to his kin," regarding Abraham, Ishmael, Isaac, Aaron, and Moses (Gen 25:8, 17; 35:29; Num 20:24; Deut 32:50). All of these expressions stem from the idea that a person is buried in the family tomb where he joins his deceased ancestors. However, according to the biblical narrative, Abraham, Aaron, and Moses were not buried with their forefathers. Despite man's perishability, there is an element that survives his death. In other words, death is a transition to the afterlife, where one is united with his ancestors. As Sarna pointed out, it was thought that the idea of the afterlife was only known in Israel in a later period, but this, evidently, is invalid.[27]

Isaac was buried by Esau and Jacob, their names appearing according to the order of their seniority. However, this is not the case with Abraham; there it states that it was Isaac and Ishmael who buried their father. It is believed that the order was reversed because Ishmael was the son of a handmaid. By mentioning that Esau and Jacob buried their father, the author passed over the dispute between the brothers. According to Genesis 49:31, Isaac was buried in the cave of Machpelah. This is not explicitly stated in chapter 35, but can be inferred from 35:27.

According to the Ramban, it was unnecessary to mention the Cave of Machpelah because Isaac resided in Hebron (v. 27), where the cave was located, and it was evident that they would not have buried him anywhere else but his father's gravesite. Isaac died at a ripe old age. Ramban further explains that (25:8) Isaac was satisfied with his days; he was fully content with each day and he had no desire for the future to bring him something new. This is a further example of God's mercy toward the righteous, that they are content with their lot and desire no luxuries. While according to the Midrash Rabbah: The Holy One, blessed He, shows the righteous in This World the reward He is accumulating for them in the World to Come. Their souls become contented and they fall asleep; i.e., they die as if falling asleep after a satisfying, relaxing experience.[28]

An examination of the biblical passages shows that Isaac lived many years based on the following facts. Jacob was ninety-one at the birth of Joseph. According to Genesis 37:2, Joseph was seventeen when he was sold into slavery, hence Jacob was one hundred and eight at this time. Isaac was sixty when Jacob was born (25:26), thus he was one hundred sixty-eight at this stage, which means that he lived twelve years after the sale of Joseph. This shows us that in recording Isaac's death the Torah does not follow chronological order.

In conclusion the stories about Jacob and Esau were probably created to explain the complex relations between Israel and Edom in later periods. The biblical story describes them as brothers which came to illustrate the close connections between the two people. The story shows how the weaker, smaller brother succeeded to dominate his older brother. The firstborn son receives a double share of his father's inheritance. In addition, it is

---

27. Sarna, *JPS Torah Commentary: Genesis*, 174.
28. *Gen. R.* 62:3.

Isaac

possible that the rights of the firstborn and the blessings were tied together; therefore, Jacob went to such great lengths to get it. Jacob was punished severely for his acts of deception. Jacob was elected by God as it was revealed to Rebekah (Gen 25:23). Nevertheless, Jacob was impatient by trying to speed up his predestined right to be Isaac's heir. For his impatience, Jacob paid heavily. From examination of the blessing that Isaac bestowed on Jacob and Esau it appears that all along his desire was to bless Jacob and to give him the most valuable of all the blessings. Isaac saved the progeny and the promise of the land for Jacob. The blessing included nationhood and national territory and many descendants. In other words, the promises that were given before to Abraham and Isaac were given to Jacob. Isaac died at the age of one hundred and eighty and was buried by his sons in the Cave of Machpelah, where the patriarchs and matriarchs are buried. He died old and contented.

Conclusion

Isaac, the second patriarch, was the miracle child. His mother, Sarah, was barren, but when she was ninety years old and his father, Abraham, was one hundred, he was born. His birth is described in an elaborate way, depicting the events that led to his birth. In addition, we are informed of the birth of Abraham's firstborn son, Ishmael. The mention of the birth of Ishmael and the birth of Isaac has one purpose, to show that Isaac is the true heir of the Abrahamic covenant. Isaac was born as a result of God's involvement, while Ishmael was born as a result of human interference. The stories come to explain the origin of the Ishmaelites and Israelites. The banishment of Ishmael comes to legitimize Isaac as the true heir to the Abrahamic covenant. Through Isaac, the line of Abraham continues.

In the story of the binding of Isaac, Abraham is the object of the test. Isaac plays a passive role—he is overshadowed by his father. Furthermore, in the Midrashim, Isaac is portrayed as a willing victim. The story is not transitional between human sacrifice and animal sacrifice. Instead it tells the believer that human sacrifice is not the right way of worship. By Abraham passing the test it shows his obedience to and love for God; it is a sign of the strength of his faith. Abraham's love and trust in God serve as models for other nations.

Isaac's passivity is also manifested in the story of his marriage. In this story, Abraham and the servant set the events that leads to Isaac's marriage. The story is a fulfillment of the "theme call" and promise which is found in the Abrahamic narrative. God's providence and guiding hand are behind the scenes. By taking Rebekah as his wife, Isaac becomes the sole heir to the Abrahamic covenant. The promises of many descendants and the inheritance of land can be now be fulfilled. The story serves as a bridge between Abraham and Jacob, reflecting the customs and daily lives of the patriarchs of ancient times.

Conclusion

Similarly, religious practices that are mentioned in Isaac's story point to the earlier period of the patriarchs. There are no temples, priests, or regular patterns of worship. The religious customs materialize as a reaction to a developing situation. Altars are built to commemorate God's theophany. There is no mention of sacrifices. Prayers and swearing are simple, spontaneous outpourings of the heart and are not connected to a physical site or a cult. They are individual and tailored for a specific purpose. Blessings are pronounced by God, but also by individuals. Isaac is the first patriarch that blesses his sons. He is also the first person who is circumcised at eight days old. In Genesis, all of Abraham's descendants are circumcised. The custom of circumcision was an ancient one and was also practiced by the Egyptians. Reading Isaac's stories shows there is no religious antagonism with the local population. There is no mention of conflict with idolatry. Furthermore, there appears to be no major differences between the religious beliefs of the patriarch Isaac and his neighbors. The religious customs which appear in Genesis point to a distinctly primitive stage of the Israelite religion. Differences of beliefs between the Israelites and their neighbors become more apparent only after the covenant at Sinai.

Isaac is connected with places such as Beer-lehi-roi and Beer-sheba, where the local deities, "El Roi" and "El Olam," are worshipped. Since he lived in those areas, it appears that he was familiar with those *elim* and worshipped them. Isaac is also mentioned as worshipping "the God of the Father" (Gen 26:24). Another deity that is mentioned with Isaac is the "Fear of Isaac" (31:42; 53), a god whose powers sent terror among all of his enemies. Isaac did not worship many gods. Isaac selected a name for God that matched his particular need at that moment in time. Each name and phrase had a different meaning and referred to God's different attributes. In two separate incidents, we read that Yahweh appeared to Isaac (26:2, 24). One of the ways God appeared to humans was through the medium of dreams, thus, we believe the second theophany Isaac received was in the form of a dream (26:24). Another form of God's manifestation, which is typical to the patriarchal narrative and to the judges' period, is the appearance of angels. Hence, we read of angels' appearances in the stories about Ishmael and Isaac. The unclear distinction between God and angels led scholars to infer that the angel was not an independent being but a manifestation of divine power and will.

Chapter 26 covers the main Isaac tradition, painting a picture of Isaac's life in general. The patriarch appears here as the main character. It

CONCLUSION

describes his agricultural venture, successes in digging wells, and his feuds with Abimelech, the king of Gerar. Isaac exemplified the natural process of nomads in the ancient world who changed from nomads to farmers. Scholars note that the stories about Isaac and Abraham share many similar elements. Indeed, the narrator borrows some of the stories from the Abrahamic cycle and creates one story by adding new dimensions to it. An examination of the Isaac story reveals it is more developed and cohesive, in contrast to the Abrahamic cycle, which is fragmented. The individual episodes have knowledge of the previous episodes, which produce a unified work. The chapter describes the events in Isaac's life prior to the birth of his sons. It refers to different events that took place in the life of the patriarch. The chapter demonstrates the fulfillment of the promises that were given to Abraham. Isaac is the true heir to Abraham and he is an individual in his own right.

Chapter 26 also includes a story about Isaac, that while staying in Gerar he deceived Abimelech, the local king, and passed off his wife, Rebekah, as his sister. The story is similar to two previous stories where the patriarch Abraham referred to his wife Sarah as his sister (12:10–20; 20). Furthermore, in chapter 20, the name of the king who was deceived is Abimelech. Analysis of these stories shows there is progressive development in these stories. Story version B has several features, which indicates that the author of B had previous knowledge of version A. Furthermore, in version B, we find answers to some of the questions that were left open in version A. In version C, we find elements from both stories A and B. This is not a coincidence since repetition is a well-known technique used by the biblical narrator and is found many times in the literature of the ancient world. By repeating the stories, while adding or subtracting details, the narrator wanted to stress a point. The audience was already familiar with the stories and their outcome and enjoyed hearing the story over and over again. The narrator would alter and change some of the story's motifs, but would preserve its core by using similar words and expressions. During the process of their incorporation into the book of Genesis the three accounts were modified in light of each other. The story in version C was altered in order to show the parallels between the lives of Abraham and Isaac. It is missing moral and theological questions regarding the wife-sister deception. It is clearly an artificial literary tradition about Isaac based directly on the traditions of Abraham. Although God is not mentioned here, the sense is that God is behind the scene, for, just as he rescued Abraham, he

Conclusion

does so with Isaac. An examination of the three versions shows that they are organized chronologically. Version A is the most ancient one. Version B appeared later and is based on version A. Version C is the latest version based on the previous two.

Since his wife Rebekah was barren, Isaac prayed to God to open her womb. His prayers were answered and Rebekah became pregnant with twins. It is suggested that the stories about Jacob and Esau were probably created in some later period in order to explain the complex relations between Israel and Edom. On the other hand, there are scholars who reject the idea that the relationship between Jacob and Esau reflects the future relationship between Israel and Edom. However, according to Noth, the intent of the Jacob-Esau story is to exhibit that the herdsman receives preference over the huntsman. The herdsman thinks he is entitled to receive preference, so he achieves it by the stupidity of the huntsman and by his own cleverness and craftiness. However, nowhere in the earlier stories of Jacob and Esau is Jacob described as a herdsman. More than likely the story comes to show how the weaker and the smaller brother succeeded in dominating his older brother. This motif, where the younger brother surpasses his older brother, is prevalent in the biblical narrative. Later in life, Isaac became old and blind. In the story of his deception, Isaac is a victim of intrigue devised by Rebekah and Jacob. At first it seems Isaac did not see that Esau was unworthy of his blessing and Jacob was the worthier man. However, examination of the following chapter shows that Isaac was aware of his surroundings and Isaac saved the blessing of progeny and the promise of the land for Jacob. Nevertheless, Jacob was punished severely for his acts of deception. Isaac died at the age of one hundred eighty. He was buried at the cave of Machpelah by his sons. He lived a full life and died of natural causes at an old age.

Bibliography

Aitken, Kenneth T. "The Wooing of Rebekah: A Study in the Development of the Tradition." *JSOT* 30 (1984) 3–23.
Albright, William Foxwell. *From the Stone Age to Christianity*. Garden City, NY: Doubleday, 1957.
Alexander, T. Desmond. "Are the Wife/Sister Incidents in Genesis Literary Compositional Variants?" *VT* 42 (1992) 145–53.
———. "The Hagar Traditions in Genesis XVI and XXI." In *Studies in the Pentateuch*, edited by John A. Emerton, 131–48. VTSup 41. Leiden: Brill, 1990.
Allen, Christine Garside. "On Me Be the Curse, My Son!" In *Encounter with the Text: Form and History in the Hebrew Bible*, edited by Martin J. Buss, 159–72. Philadelphia: Fortress, 1979.
Alt, Albrecht. "The God of the Fathers." In *Essays on Old Testament History and Religion*, translated by R. A. Wilson, 3–77. Oxford: Blackwell, 1966.
Andrews, David Keith. "Yahweh the God of the Heavens." In *Seed of Wisdom: Essays in the Honor of T. J. Meek*, edited by W. Stewart McCullough, 45–57. Toronto: University of Toronto Press, 1964.
Attridge, Harold W., and Robert A. Oden, Jr. *Philo of Byblos: The Phoenician History* Washington, DC: The Catholic Biblical Association of America, 1981.
Augustine. *The City of God against the Pagan*. Translated by Eva Matthews Sanford and William McAllen Green. Cambridge, MA: Harvard University Press, 1965.
Bar, Shaul. *A Letter that has Not Been Read: Dreams in the Hebrew Bible*. Cincinnati: Hebrew Union College Press, 2001.
———. "What did the Servant Give to Rebecca's Brother and Mother?' *Bib* 94 (2013) 565–72.
Bar-Efrat, Shimon. "Some Observations on the Analysis of Structure in Biblical Narrative." *VT* 30 (1980) 154–73.
Barr, James. "Theophany and Anthropomorphism in the Old Testament." In *Congress Volume Oxford 1959*, edited by George Wishart Anderson et al., 31–38. VTSup 7. Leiden: Brill, 1960.
Blum, Erhard. *Die Komposition der Vätergeschichte*. WMANT 57. Neukirchener-Vluyn: Neukirchener, 1984.
Bright, John. *A History of Israel*. Philadelphia: Westminster, 1972.
Calvin, John. *Commentaries on the First Book of Moses Called Genesis*. Translated by John King. Grand Rapids: Eerdmans, 1948.
Cardascia, Guillaume. *Les lois assyriennes*. Paris: Cerf, 1969.

Bibliography

Carr, David M. *Reading the Fractures of Genesis: Historical and Literary Approach.* Louisville: Westminster John Knox, 1996.
Cassuto, Umberto. "Isaac." *EM* 3 (1958) 752–54.
———. *The "Quaestio" of the Book of Genesis.* Translated by Emanuele Menachem Hartom. Jerusalem: Magnes, 1990.
Clark, W. Malcolm. "A Legal Background to the Yahwist's Use of 'Good and Evil' in Genesis 2–3." *JBL* 88 (1969) 266–78.
Clines, David J. A. *What Does Eve Do to Help?* JSOTSup 94. Sheffield, UK: JSOT, 1990.
Cohen Eskenazi, Tamara, and Tikva Frymer-Kensky. *The JPS Bible Commentary: Ruth.* Philadelphia: The Jewish Publication Society, 2011.
Cohen, Jeffery M. "Was Abraham Heartless?" *JBQ* 23.3 (1995)180–81.
Cornelius, Izak. "Genesis XXVI and Mari: The Dispute Over Water and Socio-Economic Way of Life of the Patriarchs." *JNSL* 12 (1984) 53–61.
Cross, Frank Moore. *Canaanite Myth and Hebrew Epic: Essays in the History of the Religion of Israel.* Cambridge, MA: Harvard University Press, 1973.
———. "Yahweh and the God of the Patriarchs." *HTR* 55 (1962) 225–59.
Dahood, Mitchell. "The Name *yišmā'ēl* in Genesis 16, 11." *Bib* 49 (1968) 87–8.
———. *Ugaritic-Hebrew Philology.* Rome: Pontifical Biblical Institute, 1965.
Dillmann, August. *Genesis: Critically and Exegetically Expounded.* Translated by William B. Stevenson. Edinburgh: T. & T. Clark, 1897.
Driver Godfrey Rolles, and John C. Miles, eds. *The Assyrian Laws.* Oxford: Clarendon, 1935.
Eissfeldt, Otto. "Palestine in the Time of the Nineteenth Dynasty: The Exodus and Wandering." In *The Cambridge Ancient History, Volume 2,* edited by Iorwerth Eiddon Stephen Edwards, 307–30. 9 vols. Cambridge: Cambridge University Press, 1965.
Epistle of Barnabas. In *The Apostolic Fathers,* 2nd ed., edited and translated by Joseph Barber Lightfoot and John Reginald Harmer, 159–88. Grand Rapids: Baker, 1992.
Fensham, F. Charles. "The Son of a Handmaid in Northwest Semitic." *VT* 19 (1969) 312–21.
Finkelstein, Jacob J., trans. "Additional Mesopotamian Legal Documents." In *ANET* 542–47.
———. "The Laws of Ur-Nammu." In *ANET* 523–25.
Fishbane, Michael. *Text and Texture.* New York: Shocken, 1979.
Fitzmyer, Joseph A. *The Aramaic Inscription of Sefire.* BibOr 19. Rome: Pontifical Biblical Institute, 1967.
Freedman, David Noel. "The Chronology of Israel and the Ancient Near East: An Old Testament Chronology." In *The Bible and the Ancient Near East: Essays in Honor of W. F. Albright,* edited by George Ernest Wright, 203–14. London: Rutledge & Kegan Paul, 1961.
Gardiner, Alan H. "Adoption Extraordinary." *JEA* 26 (1940) 23–29.
Gerstenberger, Erhard. "עָתָר *'ātar*; עָתָר *'ātār*." *TDOT* 11 (2001) 458–60.
Giveon, Raphael. *Les Bédouins Shosou des documents égyptiens.* Leiden: Brill, 1971.
Goetze, Albrecht, trans. "Plague Prayers of Mursilis." In *ANET* 394–96.
Gordon, Cyrus H. "Biblical Customs and the Nuzu Tablets." *BA* 3 (1940) 1–12.
Gottwald, Norman K. *Tribes of Yahweh: A Sociology of Liberated Israel, 1250–1050.* Maryknoll, NY: Orbis, 1979.
Greenspahn, Frederick E. *Hapax Legomena in Biblical Hebrew.* SBLDS 74. Chico, CA: Scholars, 1984.
Gunkel, Herman. *Genesis.* Translated by Mark E. Biddle. Macon, GA: Mercer University Press, 1977.

———. *The Legends of Genesis*. Translated by William Herbert Carruth. Chicago: Open Court, 1907.
Hall, Robert G. "Circumcision." In *ABD* 1:1025–31.
Hals, Ronald M. *The Theology of the Book of Ruth*. Facet Book. Philadelphia: Fortress, 1969.
Hamilton, Victor. *The Book of Genesis, Chapters 18–50*. Grand Rapids: Eerdmans, 1995.
Haran, Menahem. "The Religion of the Patriarchs: An Attempt at a Synthesis." *ASTI* 4 (1965) 30–55.
Hendel, Ronald S. *The Epic of the Patriarch: The Jacob Cycle and the Narrative Traditions of Canaan and Israel*. Atlanta: Scholars, 1987.
Herodotus. *Histories*. Translated by Alfred Denis Godley. Cambridge, MA: Harvard University Press, 1930.
Hillers, Delbert R. "Paḥad Yiṣḥāq." *JBL* 91 (1972) 90–92.
———. *Treaty Curses and OT Prophets*. Rome: Pontifical Biblical Institute, 1964.
Hoftijzer, Jacob. *Die Verheissungen an die drei Erzväter*. Leiden: Brill, 1956.
Honeyman, Alexander Mackie. "Merismus in Biblical Hebrew." *JBL* 71 (1952) 11–18.
Hubbard, David Allan. *Joel and Amos: An Introduction and Commentary*. Leicester, UK: InterVarsity, 1989.
Hyatt, J. Philip. "Yahweh as 'The God of My Father.'" *VT* 5 (1955) 130–36.
Irenaeus. *Against the Heresies*. In *Ante-Nicene Fathers*, edited by Alexander Roberts and James Donaldson, 309–567. Grand Rapids: Eerdmans,1975.
Jacob, Benno. *The First Book of the Bible: Genesis*. New York: Ktav, 1974.
Jay, Nancy. "Sacrifice, Descent and the Patriarchs." *VT* 38 (1988) 52–70.
Jenni, Ernst. "Das Wort ʿōlām im Alten Testament." *ZAW* 64 (1952)197–248.
———. "Das Wort ʿōlām im Alten Testament." *ZAW* 65 (1953)1–35.
———. " ʿōlām." *TLOT* (1997) 2:852–62.
Josephus. *Jewish Antiquities*. Translated by Henry St. John Thackeray. Cambridge, MA: Harvard University Press, 1930.
Kalimi, Isaac. "The Land of Moriah, Mount Moriah, and the Site of Solomon's Temple in Biblical Historiography." *HTR* 83 (1990) 345–62.
Knudtzon, Jørgen Alexander. *Die El-Amarna-Tafeln*. VAB 22. 2 vols. 1915. Reprint. Aalen, Germany: Otto Zeller, 1964.
Koch, Klaus. *The Growth of the Biblical Tradition*. Translated by Susan Marianne Cupitt. New York: Charles Scribner's Sons, 1969.
———. "Pāḥăd Jiṣḥaq- eine Gottesbezeichnung? In *Werden und Wirken des Alten Testament: Festschrift für Claus Westermann zum 70 Geburstag*, edited by Rainer Albertz et al., 107–15. Göttingen: Vandenhoeck und Ruprecht, 1980.
Kramer, Samuel Noah, trans. "Lipit–Ishtar Law Code." In *ANET* 159–61.
Kugel, James L. *How to Read the Bible: A Guide to Scripture, Then and Now*. New York: Free Press, 2007.
Labuschagne, Casper J. "The našû-nadānu Formula and its Biblical Equivalent." In *Travels in the world of the Old Testament: Studies Presented to M. A. Beek*, edited by M. S. H. G. Heerma van Voss et al., 176–80. Assen, The Netherlands: Van Gorcum, 1974.
Levenson, Jon D. *The Death and Resurrection of the Beloved Son: The Transformation of the Child Sacrifice in Judaism and Christianity*. New Haven, CT: Yale University Press, 1993.
Levine, Baruch A. *In the Presence of the Lord*. Leiden: Brill, 1974.
———. *Numbers 1–20*. AB 4A. New York: Doubleday, 1993.

Bibliography

———. "paḥad yiṣḥāq." *EM* 6:451–52.
Lewy, Julius. "Les textes paléo-assyriens et l'An cien Testament." *RHR* 110 (1934) 29–65
Loewenstamm, Samuel. "Hagar." *EM* 2:782–84.
Luke, John Tracy. "Abraham and the Iron Age: Reflection on the New Patriarchal Studies." *JSOT* 4 (1977) 35–47.
Lutz, David A. "The Isaac Tradition in the Book of Genesis." PhD diss., Drew University, 1969.
Maimonides, Moses. (Rambam). *The Guide of the Perplexed*. Translated by Michael Friedländer. New York: Hebrew Publishing Co, 1881.
Malul, Meir. "More on the Paḥad Yiṣḥāq (Genesis XXXI 42, 53) and the Oath by the Thigh." *VT* 35 (1985) 192–200.
Mathews, Kenneth A. *The New American Commentary: Genesis 11:27—50:26*. Nashville: Broadman & Holman, 2005.
Matthews, Victor Harold. "The Wells of Gerar." *BA* 49 (1986) 118–26.
Mayer, Günter. "עָרֵל 'āral." *TDOT* 11:359–61.
Mazor, Yair. "Genesis 22: The Ideological Rhetoric and Psychological Composition." *Bib* 67 (1986) 81–88.
McCarter, P. Kyle, and Ronald. S. Hendel. "The Patriarchal Age: Abraham, Isaac and Jacob." In *Ancient Israel*, edited by Hershel Shanks, 1–31. Washington, DC: Biblical Archeology Society, 1999.
McCarthy, Dennis. J. "Covenant-Relationship." In *Institution and Narrative: Collected Essays*, edited by Dennis J. McCarthy, 54–66. AnBib 108. Rome: Biblical Institute, 1985.
McCree, Walter T. "The Covenant Meal in the OT." *JBL* 45 (1926) 120–28.
Meek, Theophile J., trans. "The Code Hammurabi." In *ANET* 163–80.
Midrash Sechel Tov. Buber Solomon ed. New York: Menorah, 1963.
Milgrom, Jacob. *Cult and Conscience*. Leiden: Brill, 1976.
Millard, Allan R. "Methods of Studying the Patriarchal Narratives as Ancient Texts." In *Essays on the Patriarchal Narratives*, edited by Allan R. Millard and Donald J. Wiseman, 35–51. Winona Lake, IN: Eisenbrauns, 1983.
Miller, J. Maxwell. "The Patriarchs and Extra-Biblical Sources: A Response." *JSOT* 2 (1977) 62–66.
Moran, William L. "The Scandal of the 'Great Sin' at Ugarit." *JNES* 18 (1959) 280–81.
Morgenstern, Julian. "The 'Bloody Husband' (?) (Exod. 4:24–26) Once Again." *HUCA* 34 (1963) 35–70.
———. *Rites of Birth, Marriage, Death and Kindred Occasions among the Semites*. Cincinnati: Hebrew Union College Press, 1966.
Neff, Robert Wilbur. "The Annunciation in the Birth Narrative of Ishmael." *BR* 17 (1972) 51–60.
Nemoy, Leon. *Karaite Anthology: Excerpts from Early Literature*. New Haven, CT: Yale University Press, 1952.
Nicol, George G. "The Chronology of Genesis: Genesis XXVI 1–33 as 'Flashback.'" *VT* 46 (1996) 330–38.
———. "The Narrative Structure and Interpretation of Genesis XXVI 1–33." *VT* 46 (1966) 339–60.
———. "Studies in the Interpretation of Gen. 26:1–33." PhD diss., Oxford University, 1987.

Nikaido, Scott. "Hagar and Ishmael as Literary Figures: An Intertextual Study." *VT* 51 (2001) 219–42.
North, Francis Sparling. "Four-Month Seasons of the Hebrew Bible." *VT* 11 (1961) 446–48.
Noth, Martin. *The History of Israel*. Translated by Peter. R. Ackroyd. New York: Harper & Row, 1958.
———. *A History of Pentateuchal Tradition*. Translated with an Introduction by Bernhard W. Anderson. Englewood Cliffs, NJ: Prentice-Hall, 1972.
Oppenheim, A. Leo. *The Interpretation of Dreams in the Ancient Near East: With a Translation of an Assyrian Dream Book*. Transactions of the American Philosophical Society, New Series, vol. 46. Philadelphia: American Philosophical Society, 1956.
Pardee, Dennis. "An Emendation in the Ugaritic Aqht Text." *JNES* 36 (1977) 53–56.
Pesikta Rabbati. Translated by William G. Braude. New Haven, CT: Yale University Press, 1968.
Pfeiffer, Robert H., trans. "Oracles Concerning Esarhaddon." In *ANET* 449–50.
Pinker, Aron. "The Expulsion of Hagar and Ishmael (Gen 21:9–21)." *Women and Judaism* 6 (2009) 1–24.
Pitard, Wayne T. "Before Israel: Syria-Palestine in the Bronze Age." In *The Oxford History of the Biblical World*, edited by Michael D. Cogan, 33–77. Oxford: Oxford University Press, 1998.
Pritchard, James B., ed. *Ancient Near Eastern Texts Reading Relating to the Old Testament*. 3rd ed. with Supplement. Princeton, NJ: Princeton University Press, 1969.
de Pury, Albert. "EL- OLAM." In *DDD*, 288–91.
———. *Promesse divine et légende cultuelle dans le cycle de Jacob, Genèse 28 et les traditions patriarchales*. Études bibliques. Paris: Gabalda 1975.
Rabinowitz, Jacob. J. "The 'Great Sin' in Ancient Egyptian Marriage Contracts." *JNES* 18 (1959) 73.
von Rad, Gerhard. *Genesis: A Commentary*. Translated by John H. Marks. Philadelphia: Westminster, 1961.
———. "Josephsgeschite und ältere Chokma." *VTSup* 1 (1953) 120–27.
Rendsburg, Gary A. "Some False Leads in the Identification of Late Biblical Hebrew Texts: The Case of Genesis 24 and 1 Samuel 2:27–36." *JBL* 121 (2002) 23–46
Rofé, Alexander. "La composizione di Gen.24." *BeO* 23 (1981) 161–65.
———. "Sippur 'Erusei Rivqa (Bereshit 24) Meḥqar Sifruti-Histori." *Eshel Beer-Sheva* 1 (1976) 42–67.
Rowley, Harold Henry. *The Faith of Israel*. London: SCM, 1956.
Safren, Jonathan D. "Ahuzzath and the Pact of Beer-Sheba." *ZAW* 101 (1989) 184–98.
Sarna, Nahum M. *Exploring Exodus: The Heritage of Biblical Israel*. New York: Schocken, 1986.
———. *The JPS Torah Commentary: Genesis*. Philadelphia: Jewish Publication Society, 1989.
———. *Understanding Genesis*. New York: Schocken, 1966.
Sarna, Nahum M. and S. David Sperling, "Isaac." In *EncJud* 10:32–33.
Sasson, Jack M. "Circumcision in the Ancient Near East." *JBL* 85 (1966) 473–76.
Schmitt, John J. "Virgin." In *ABD* 6:853–54.
Segal, Moses Hirsch. "The Religion of Israel before Sinai." *Tarbiz* 30 (1961) 215–30.
Selman, Martin J. "Comparative Customs and the Patriarchal Age." In *Essays on the Patriarchal Narratives*, edited by Allan R. Millard and Donald J. Wiseman, 91–139. Winona Lake, IN: Eisenbrauns, 1983.

Bibliography

Simonis, Johann, and Johann G. Eichhorn. *Lexicon Manuale Hebraicum et Chaldaicum in Veteris Testamenti Libros*. Edited by Georg Benedikt Winer. 4th ed. Leipzig: Fleischer, 1828.

Singer, Itamar. "Sea Peoples." In *ABD* 5 (1992) 1059–61.

Skinner, John. *A Critical and Exegetical Commentary on Genesis*. ICC. New York: Charles Scribner's Sons, 1910.

Speiser, Ephraim Avigdor. *Genesis*. AB 1. Garden City, NY: Doubleday, 1964.

———. "The Wife-Sister Motif in the Patriarchal Narratives." In *Oriental and Biblical Studies Collected Writings of E. A. Speiser*, edited by Jacob. J. Finkelstein and Moshe Greenberg, 62–82. Philadelphia: University of Pennsylvania Press, 1967.

Stamm, Johann Jakob. "Der Name Isaak." In *Festschrift für A. Schädelin*, edited by Hans Dürr and Wilhelm Michaelis, 33–38. Bern: Herbert Lang, 1950.

Talmon, Shemaryahu. "The 'Comparative Method,' in Biblical Interpretation: Principles and Problems." In Congress Volume *VTSup*, 29, edited by John. A. Emerton et al., 320–56. Leiden: Brill, 1977.

Thompson, John L. "Hagar, Victim or Villain? Three Sixteenth-Century Views." *CBQ* 59 (1997) 213–33.

Thompson, Thomas L. *The Historicity of the Patriarchal Narratives: The Quest for the Historical Abraham*. BZAW 133. Berlin: de Gruyter, 1974.

———. *The Origin Tradition of Ancient Israel I: The Literary Formation of Genesis and Exodus 1–23*. JSOTSup 55. Sheffield: JSOT, 1987.

Towner, W. Sibley. "'Blessed be Yahweh' and 'Blessed Art Thou, Yahweh': The Modulation of a Biblical Formula.'" *CBQ* 30 (1968) 388–89.

Tsevat, Matitiahu. "Bᵉkhôr." In *TDOT* 2:121–27.

———. *The Meaning of the Book of Job and Other Biblical Studies*. New York: Ktav, 1980.

Vall, Gregory. "What Was Isaac Doing in the Field (Genesis XXIV 63)?" *VT* 44 (1994) 513–23.

Van Selms, Adrianus. "Isaac in Amos." In *Studies on the Books of Hosea and Amos: Papers read at the 7th and 8th meetings of Die O.T. Werkgemeenskap in Suid-Afrika 1964–1965*, edited by Society for the Study of the Old Testament in South Africa, 157–65. Potchefstroom: Pro Rege-Pers Beperk.

Van Seters, John. *Abraham in History and Tradition*. New Haven, CT: Yale University Press, 1975.

———. *Prologue to History: The Yahwist as Historian in Genesis*. Louisville: Westminster John Knox, 1992.

———. "The Religion of the Patriarchs in Genesis." *Bib* 61 (1980) 220–33.

de Vaux, Roland. *Ancient Israel: Its Life and Institutions*. Translated by John Mchugh. London: Darton, Longman & Todd, 1961.

———. *The Early History of Israel*. Translated by David Smith. Philadelphia: Westminster, 1978.

Vawter, Bruce. *On Genesis: A New Reading*. Garden City, NY: Doubleday, 1977.

Warner, Sean M. "The Patriarchs and Extra-Biblical Sources." *JSOT* 2 (1977) 50–61

Watson, Wilfred G. E. "The Falcon Episode in the Aqhat Tale." *JNSL* 5(1977) 69–75.

Wellhausen, Julius. *Prolegomena to the History of Israel*. Translated by Allan Menzies and John Sutherland Black. Edinburgh: Adam & Charles Black, 1885.

Wenham, Gordon J. "Betûlāh: 'A Girl of Marriageable Age.'" *VT* 22 (1972) 326–48.

———. *Genesis 16–50*. WBC 2. Nashville: Thomas Nelson, 2000.

---. "The Religion of the Patriarchs." In *Essays on the Patriarchal Narratives,* edited by Allan R. Millard and Donald J. Wiseman, 161–95. Winona Lake, IN: Eisenbrauns, 1983.

Westermann, Claus. *Genesis 12–36: A Commentary.* Translated by John J. Scullion. Minneapolis: Augsburg, 1985.

---. *The Promises to the Fathers.* Translated by David E. Green. Philadelphia: Fortress, 1980.

Index

HEBREW BIBLE

Genesis
 xv, xix, xx, xxi, 1, 36, 53, 54, 58, 62, 63, 64, 68, 68n11, 72, 74, 83, 85, 110

1:22	60
1:28	60
2:4	65
3	4
3:9	5
3:24	12
4:3	34
4:9	5
4:14	12
6:11, 13	4
6:13–21	73
8:20	34
10:9	17
11:26	2
11:30	2
12	73, 98, 99, 101, 111
12:1	22, 65, 73
12:1–3	49
12:2	2
12:2–3, 7	123
12:3	85
12:4–5	100
12:7	54, 73, 74
12:7, 8	27
12:8	54, 58
12:10	81, 85, 93, 99, 110
12:10–13	106
12:10–20	xxii, 34, 98, 99, 129
12:11	22
12:11–13	99
12:11–15	106
12:12	110
12:13	107
12:14–16	100
12:16	3, 86, 110, 119
12:17	110
12:17–20	100
12:18	107
12:19	99
12:20	87, 94
13	100
13:2	86, 108, 110
13:2–10	96
13:4	54, 58
13:8–9	88
13:11–12	96
13:14–17	96
13:15, 17	123
13:18	27, 54, 96
14	96
14:18–22	66
14:19–20	97
14:22	39, 68
15	2, 17
15:1	70n15
15:2	40
15:3–4	7
15:4	9
15:5	2
15:7–8, 18	123
15:8	40
15:13–21	73
16	15, 17, 34

Index

Genesis (*continued*)

16: 7, 9, 10, 11	5
16:1–4	15
16:1–14	16
16:1–16	15
16:1a, 3, 15–16	16
16:2	16
16:2–3	4
16:3	67
16:4	12
16:7, 9, 10, 11	77–78
16:7–9, 11	78
16:8	5
16:9	7, 16
16:10	18
16:11	5, 15, 16
16:12	17
16:13	15, 66, 68, 78
16:14	13, 66
16:15–16	7
16:16	16
16:18	15
17	63, 73
17:1	2, 66, 73, 74
17:1, 6, 8, 16, 20	123
17:2	2, 5
17:4–6	9, 18
17:7, 23	18
17:9–14	61
17:12	11, 62
17:15–21	73
17:16	8
17:16–21	9
17:17	11
17:18	9
17:19	1, 8, 11, 62
17:20	14
17:21	10, 61
18	73
18:1	73, 74
18:1, 16, 22	77
18:2–7	41
18:10	9, 10
18:11, 12, 13	8
18:12	1, 8
18:13	22
18:17	73
18:18	85
18:23	102
18:25	21
19:1, 15	77
19:2	22
19:5, 9	77
19:5, 10, 12, 16	77
20	xxii, 10, 82, 83, 98, 99, 100, 111, 129
20:2	82, 100, 104, 106, 107
20:2–18	99
20:3	75, 101, 102
20:3–7	101
20:4	102
20:4–5	102
20:6	101
20:6–7	102
20:7	56, 102
20:8	102, 106
20:9	107
20:11	100, 105
20:13	100, 106
20:15	86, 105
20:17	56, 101
21	15, 17, 20, 89
21:1	9
21:1–7	xv
21:1–21	15, 16
21:2	1, 10, 52
21:5	16
21:6	1, 8
21:6b	11
21:7	11
21:8–14	xv
21:8–21	15
21:9–21	5
21:10–19	16
21:12	16, 18
21:13	14
21:14	13
21:17	16, 28, 78
21:20	15, 17
21:22	89
21:22 LXX	89
21:22–32	90
21:22–34	91
21:23	59

Index

21:25	88, 93	24:11–48	49
21:25–30	86	24:12	44, 51, 57
21:28–29	92	24:12–14	57
21:32	89	24:14	41
21:32 LXX	89	24:15–27	37
21:33	58, 66, 67, 76, 92	24:16	41, 44, 104
22	xx, 20, 23, 28	24:19–20	41
22:1, 7, 11	21	24:20	xv
22:1, 11–18	78	24:22–23	44
22:1–19	xv, 23	24:25	44
22:2	22, 23, 49, 55	24:26–27	57
22:6	25, 27	24:27	51, 57
22:7	21, 29	24:28–61	37
22:8	27, 29, 35	24:31	43
22:10	31	24:34–49	44
22:11	21, 24	24:35	44, 49, 86
22:11, 15	5	24:36	18
22:12	21, 23	24:38	44
22:13	35, 55	24:39	44
22:14	23, 29	24:42	44
22:14b	35	24:43	44
22:15	29	24:47	45
22:17	5, 47, 49, 60, 123	24:48	45
22:18	85	24:50–51	50
22:19	33	24:53, 55	45
23:2	47	24:54	46
24	xxi, 37, 43, 49, 50, 51, 52	24:55	46
		24:57	52
24:1, 35	49	24:58	47
24:1–9	37	24:59–60	52
24:1–27	44	24:60	47, 49, 60
24:3	39, 59	24:62	6, 47, 67
24:3, 7, 8, 41	49	24:62–63	66
24:4	44	24:62–67	xv, 37
24:4, 7	50	24:65	47
24:4–7	49	25	95, 104, 117
24:5	39	25:5	18, 52
24:5, 7	49	25:6	15, 18
24:7	39, 44, 123	25:7	47
24:7 LXX	39	25:8	123, 124, 125
24:7–8	40	25:8, 17	124
24:8	44	25:9–11	xv
24:9	71	25:11	61, 67
24:10	18	25:12–18	5
24:10–14	37	25:18	6
24:11	66	25:19	10, 11
24:11–16	46	25:19–28	xv

Index

Genesis (*continued*)

25:20–34	95
25:21	57
25:22	114
25:23	58, 115, 122, 123, 126
25:26	125
25:27—34:27	117
25:29–34	115, 121
25–32	49
25:34	119
26	xv, xvi, xxii, 79, 80, 81, 83, 87, 89, 96, 97, 98, 99, 103, 111, 128, 129
26:1	81, 82, 93
26:1–11	81, 95, 98
26:1–33	81, 95, 96, 97
26:2	73, 74
26:2, 24	74, 79, 128
26:3	55, 74, 85, 86, 90, 91, 96, 108
26:3–4, 24	123
26:4	85
26:5	xvii
26:6	87
26:7	104
26:7–9	xvi
26:7–11	90, 96
26:8	104
26:9	104, 107
26:10	107
26:11	96, 104
26:12	84, 86
26:12–13	108
26:12–13, 29	52
26:12–16, 17–23	96
26:12–22	96
26:12–33	81, 95
26:13	86, 91
26:14	84, 86
26:15, 18	86, 93
26:16	91
26:16, 26–32	96
26:17	86, 87
26:18	84, 92
26:19–20, 25, 32	84
26:20	87
26:21	87
26:22	87
26:23	87, 96
26:23–25a	76
26:24	5, 69, 73, 75, 76, 79, 96, 128
26:25	54, 58, 84, 92, 96
26:26–31	97
26:27–50	96
26:28–29	96
26:29	91, 97
26:30	90
26:31	59
27	xv, 95, 115, 117
27:1–29	xvi
27:2	17
27:4	121
27:20	121
27:24	121
27:28	86
27:32	121
27:33	121
27:33–37	xvi
27:34	121
27:35	122
27:40	115, 122, 123
27:46	114
28:1–4	56
28:3	66
28:10–22	7
28:11	75
28:12	77, 78
28:12–18	73
28:12–19	68
28:13	69, 70, 75, 79
28:13 LXX	76
28:14	85
29	43
29:1–14	52
29:2–14	49
29:6, 9	46
29:10–11	42
29:23–25	48
29:24, 29	47
30:14	86
30:31–43	121
30:43	86
31:5, 29	69

31:10–13	73
31:13	66, 75
31:22	25
31:24	75
31:24, 29	72
31:42	72
31:42, 53	70, 71, 79, 128
32:4	77
32:5, 15	86
32:14–22	121
32:20	73
32:25–30	73
33	95
33:1–2	77
33:18	87
33:20	66
34	62, 95, 123
34:4	38
34:25	4
35	95, 124, 125
35:1	55
35:7	66
35:8	47
35:9	73
35:11	66
35:16–20	123
35:27	125
35:27–29	xv, xvi, xxiii, 124
35:28	124
35:29	123, 124
36:7	86
37:2	125
37:7	86
41:25	109
41–47	81
43:1	110
43:13	66
43:23	69
46:1	55, 69, 92
46:1–4	73
46:3	69, 76
47:4	85
47:9	123
47:30	124
48:3	66
48:9–20	56
49:3	118
49:3–28	56
49:5	4
49:24	70
49:25	66
49:26	69
49:31	xvi, 125
50:24–25	9

Exodus

	65, 66
1:7	87
1:16	110
2	43
2:16–22	42
3:2	78
3:6	69, 79
3:18	25
3:21–22	110
4:24–26	61
4:25	61
4:31	9
6:2–3	65
6:8	59n17
8:4, 5, 24, 25, 26	57n12
9:28	57n12
10:17	57n12
11:1	110
11:2–3	110
12:35–36	110
12:48	62
13:17	82
13:21	78
14:2	87
14:9	78
15:22f	15, 25
15:25	21
16:4	21
17:15	55
18:10–11	90n30
19	23
19:2	87
20:7	109
21:17	120
22:28	56, 118
24:5	56
28–29	55
33:20	74n30
34:16	39

INDEX

Exodus (*continued*)
34:26	56
34:34	103n14

Leviticus
8–10	55
14:19	102n10
14:20	24
17:8	24
18, 21	34
18:6	102n10
19:14	120
20:2	34
21:7	48n40
21:7, 14	12
22:13	12

Numbers
8:2–26	56
8:18	56
12:6–8	74n30
12:13	56, 101
14:30	59n17
20:24	124
22:20	75
25	39
33:5–49	87

Deuteronomy
7:3	39
8:2, 16	21
11:13–17	82
12:2	23
12:31	34
21:15–17	18
21:17	118
22:14	102n10
22:19, 29	12
22:22	101
23:8	116
24:1, 3	12
27:18	120
30:19	39
31:16	124
32:40	59n17
32:50	124

Joshua
2:9–11	90n30
5:2	61
5:2–9	63
22:23	24

Judges
	83
6:11	78
6:24	55
6:26	24
6:29	58n13
8:30	82n13
11	35
11:31	24
13:3	5
13:6	77
13:20	77
14:2	38
15:1	9
19:29	26

1 Samuel
	83
1:22–24	12
6	110
9:9	58n13
11:7	72
13:9	24
14:6	62
14:8–12	41
14:50	90
17:26, 36	62
18:17–27	46n26
26:5	90
31:4	62

2 Samuel
7:12	124
8:14	115
10:18	90
24:15	102n11

1 Kings
	124
3:5	75
14:5	58n13
17:20–22	101
18:24	58
19:3	92
22:5, 8	58n13

Index

2 Kings

	124
1:2	58n13
3:11	58n13
3:27	35
4:14	10
4:33–35	101
4:38–41	118n14
5:11	58
8:8	58n13
8:20	123
8:20–22	115
14:7	115
16:3	35
16:6	116, 123
22:13, 18	58n13
23:10	35

Isaiah

1:2	39
2:3	23n6
2:10	72
8:3	102n10
12:4	58
19:3	58n13
19:8	72
24:18	71
29:1–8	35
30:29	23n6
32:14	6n11
40–46	xviii
41:8	31
49:26	70n16
52:1	62
60:16	70n16
64:6	58

Jeremiah

8:3(4)	122
9:3	123
14:6	6n11
14:12	24
21:2	58n13
29:19	9
33:26	xvii
34:9, 16	12
37:7	58n13
48:43	71

Ezekiel

14:3, 7	58n13
20:23	59n17
28:10	62
31:18	62
32:17–32	62
43:24	24
44:7, 9	62

Hosea

1:8	12
3:5	72
8:9	6n11
12:3	123
12:4(3)	122

Joel

3:5	58

Amos

	xvii
5:5	xvii, 55, 92
5:5–6	69
7:9	69
7:9, 16	xvii
8:14	xvii, 55, 69, 92

Jonah

1:9	39n6

Micah

4:2	23n6
6:6–7	35

Zephaniah

3:9	58

Haggai

1:13	77

Zechariah

8:3	23n6
13:9	58

Malachi

2:7	77
2:16	12
22:13	12

Psalms

2:11	72
13:2, 5	70n16
24:3	23n6

Psalms (continued)

34:1	82
80:19	58
91:5	71
105:1	58
105:9	xvii
116:13, 17	58
116:14	58

Proverbs

3:25	71
30:14	27

Job

1:9	21
8:3	21
15:21	71
22:10	71
24:15	103n14
39:5-8	6n11
39:22	71
42:8	56

Song of Solomon

3:8	71

Ruth

1:6	9
2:3	51
2:20	51
4:11-12	47

Lamentations

3:55	58

Esther

4:1	121

Ezra

1:2	39n6
1:6	46
4:6	88
10:44	49

Nehemiah

1:4	39n6
1:5	39n6
2:4	39n6
2:20	39n6

1 Chronicles

1:28	10
1:34	10
16:16	xvii
34:21, 26	58n13

2 Chronicles

	124
3:1	22
11:22	49
13:21	49
20:16	35
21:3	46
24:3	49
25:11-12	115
36:23	39n6

ANCIENT NEAR EASTERN TEXTS

Arslan Tash	67
Code of Hammurabi	3, 3n3
Laws of Ur-Nammu	4n8
Lipit-Ishtar Law Code	13
Middle Assyrian Laws	103

DEUTEROCANONICAL BOOKS

2 Maccabees

7:27	12n33

PSEUDEPIGRAPHA (OLD TESTAMENT)

Jubilees

17:4	12
17:15-16	30n35

ANCIENT JEWISH WRITERS

Josephus

30

Jewish Antiquities

1:232	30n36
1.12.2	24n13

INDEX

Philo	63, 63n28
Pseudo-Philo	
Biblical Antiquities	31

RABBINIC WORKS
Talmud

Bava Kamma	
9a	88n26
Bava Metzia	
14a	88n26
31b	75n31
87a	11
Gittin	
75b	12n34
Hullin	
55b, 58b	118n17
95b	41
Ketubot	
57b	46n28
60a	12n34
93a	88n26
Kiddushin	
29a	62n25
41a	47n30
Makkot	
18b	45n21
24a	121n24
Middot	
2:5	25n15
Pesahim	
4a	24n11
56a	121n23
Roš Haššanah	
16b	8n21
Sanhedrin	
76b	113n1
89b	22n3
105b	24n12
Shabbat	
24:3	118n17
30b	61n21
54a	28n27
155b	118n17

Shevu'ot	
31a	88n26
Yevamot	
64a	3n2

Midrash

Genesis Rabbah	
	26, 30–31, 89
42:8	62n24
45:1	3n1
45:4	4n7
45:5	4n9
55:4	31n38
55:6	25n16
55:7	22n3, 22n4, 22n5, 23n10
56:1	26n17
56:2	26n21
56:3	26n23
56:4	27n25
56:8	30n35, 31n40
56:11	29n33, 33n46
60:14	48
61:6	61n20
62:3	125n28
64:6	85n18
64:9	89n28
67:4	121n26
68:11	121n23
Exodus Rabbah	
1:1	13
3:6	73n27
Leviticus Rabbah	
	31
Midrash Sechel Tov	
11	7, 7n16
Midrash *(continued)*	
Pesikta Rabbati	28, 28n29
Pirkei De-Rabbi Eliezer	27
	26n18, 27n26
Ruth Rabbah	
1.4	82n10

Index

Sifre to Deuteronomy
32   31

Tanhuma Toledot
10   121n25

Targumim

Targum for Ruth   82
Targum Neofiti   48
Targum Onkelos   6, 46, 48, 122
Targum Pseudo-Jonathan
   33, 48, 61, 122

MEDIEVAL COMMENTATORS

Abarvanel   4, 119
Bekhor Shor   6
Gersonides (Levi ben Gershon)   8
Ibn Ezra   6
Malbim   40
Nahmanides   4, 9
R' Bachya   42
Radak (Rabbi David Kimhi)   4, 6
Ramban (Nachmanides)   18, 42, 49, 82, 125
Rashbam (Samuel ben Meir)
   82, 103
Rashi (Shlomo ben Isaac)   4, 11, 21, 23, 25, 28, 39, 42, 46
Sforno (Obadja Sforno)   25, 40

Kabbalah

Zohar   41

NEW TESTAMENT

Luke
1:7   10
1:31   6

Romans
8:31–32   32n43

Galatians
4:29   12

Hebrews
11:17–19   26

EARLY CHRISTIAN WRITINGS

Augustine
City of God
16.32   33n45

1 Clement   30
31:2–4   30n37

Epistle of Barnabas
7:3   32

Irenaeus
Against the Heresies
4.5.4   32, 32n44

GRECO-ROMAN LITERATURE

Herodotus
Histories
2.37   62n27

www.ingramcontent.com/pod-product-compliance
Lightning Source LLC
Chambersburg PA
CBHW062003180426
43198CB00036B/2167